DATE DUE

GAYLORD

D1126563

WONDER IN GOD'S WILDERNESS

By

Samuel John Schmiechen

Illustrated by

Abigail Bahnemann

AUGSBURG PUBLISHING HOUSE

Minneapolis, Minnesota

WONDER IN GOD'S WILDERNESS

Manufactured in the United States of America

Preface

Nature has been the source of man's physical sustenance as well as the object of much of his religious and philosophical speculation. Primitive man, superstitious and fearsome, imagined that good and evil spirits dwelt among trees, rocks, and waters. In all ages there were those who enjoyed or exploited the earth and its treasures with or without reference to an ultimate purpose. Today some presuppose that nature is simply a cosmic machine which is sustained by eternal perpetual motion or a series of processes. Many put their faith in science, claiming it is only a matter of time before a total meaning of nature is provided. Another point of view regards man as a creature belonging exclusively within the order of nature. Others contend that nature is God and God is nature and ignore the possibility of a Being infinite beyond human thought and the myriads of universes in creation.

The artificiality, anxiety, and aimlessness of much of modern life awakens hungers which for many may be allayed among lakes and streams, forests and hills of the wilderness. The richest blessings of nature are not confined to physical recreation. Exhilaration for the inner man and new perspec-

iii

tive for the mind are proportionate to responsiveness of soul and to a capacity to interpret by faith.

The Bible approaches nature through faith in the reality of God the Creator. It is he who gives meaning to all and whom everything must glorify. "The heavens are telling the glory of God; and the firmament proclaims his handiwork" (Psalm 19:1). The God who has made the minutest particles and the vastnesses of interstellar space is the same who fashioned man in his own image.

Man's continual problem arises out of the very capacities which set him apart from all other living things. He is aware of the universe in which he lives, may explore it and may have dominion over portions of it. But what is entrusted to him as a gift tempts him to "worship and serve the creature rather than the Creator, who is blessed forever" (Rom. 1:24). What can man then do when he hears no river murmur, "I shall quiet your conscience"; no tree whisper, "Thy sins are forgiven"; no clouds give assurance, "Because I live ye shall live also"? Was God's creation finished or is it ever finished? Is God still the Lord of creation? Does he have another word to speak to man and creation?

The Apostle John gives us a clue on how the New Testament interprets life when he says that God's meaningful and saving "Word became flesh and dwelt among us, full of grace and truth" (John 1:14). He emphasizes that we are not to forget the indispensable and concomitant fact: "He was in the beginning with God; all things were made through him, and without him was not anything made that was made" (John 1:2-3). That the Creator is also our Redeemer and Lord is the key to a Christian interpretation of nature and of all life. God is not only the Father of creation and of all mankind but also the "God and Father of our Lord Jesus Christ" (Rom. 15:6).

Such enlarging and joyous awareness puts a new light upon the mystery, wisdom, and creativity of God's Spirit pervading all the earth, all history, and all existence. The impartiality and dependability of nature expose pretense and superficiality. The seasons of the year with their rhythm, fruits, and purposes evoke sobering reflections upon the transciency of life and upon the judgments of God. Every evidence of providence and of beauty hints at the constants of faith and the lovingkindness of the Eternal. Should not the testimony of our senses join our inner being to affirm, "O Lord, how manifold are thy works! In wisdom hast thou made them all" (Psalm 104:24)?

I have cherished deeply a kinship of wonder in creation with the members of St. Paul's Church.

Our daughter, Abigail Bahnemann, illustrated this book and I am grateful to her for highlighting vividly the setting of the meditations.

I cannot express with words how beholden I am to my wife Marie for a mutual love of nature, for an adventurous spirit in unconventional expeditions, and for encouragement as well as for constructive suggestions in the writing of these meditations.

SAMUEL J. SCHMIECHEN

Contents

To | Daniel

Peter

Abigail

THE CRY OF THE WILD

To hear the loon's cry of ecstasy resound from wilderness lake to forest is an eerie experience never forgotten. The quick, alternatingly low and high notes, like those of a mad clarinetist, are like no other sounds and hold one with a haunting fascination. The "take-off" for flight when feet and wings beat the water is a staccato accompaniment for this true "cry of the wild."

The weird call of the loons expresses a sense of sheer joy and abandon in the wilderness. Their cry finds a strange echo of the primitive within oneself. The sounds awaken a racial memory of belonging to this creation which God saw and called "very good." Yet as a human being one cannot react to all the surrounding breathtaking beauty with the same abandon as the bird. Man has not always consciously cooperated with nature as the bird does instinctively. Man also knows that he needs something more than the physical beauty of nature around him through which to express his life and joy. Instinctively man draws away from the cries of the wild not out of fear, but because he knows this cry is limited to uncontrolled urges of physical existence. It does not satisfy all the hungers of the heart. The howling of the wolf, the screech of the bobcat, the hoot of the owl, the scream of the eagle—all join the loon in voicing hungers and satisfactions in their elemental stages.

1

Under night skies when some of the plaintive calls of the wilderness echo mysteriously from bay and open waters, they emphasize our kinship with as well as our apartness from nature. Our spirit yearns to commune with God's Spirit. In the fourth century A.D. a brilliant young man heeded only the wild cry of his physical desires, ignored the laws of the Spirit, and soon tired of life in a wilderness of sin. He found true human nature in the nature of Christ and said, "Thou hast made us for thyself and our souls are restless until they find rest in thee."

Christ lived in a physical body among us and never despised it. Nor did he regard the instincts and desires of the body as evil in themselves. He taught us to pray for "daily bread" and had faith that our heavenly Father knows our needs. Those who were quick to condemn the sins which came to physical expression were informed that thought and lust for evil begin with the intent of mind and heart and will (Matt. 5:28). The quick and easy division of the physical or material as unspiritual and the matters of the soul as spiritual is false. Both body and soul were created to serve the good and joyful purposes ordained by God. Man may respond to the instinctive and physical "cry of the wild," but he also may hear a voice which can tame his inner nature and bring mastery and consecration for body and soul in a higher quality of life relationships. It is the voice of the Spirit that hovered over the waters at creation and the voice of the same Spirit which lives so fully in Christ. All who listen may hear it!

It is the Spirit himself bearing witness with our spirit that we are children of God (Rom. 8:16).

SCRIPTURE READING: Romans 8:12-17

PRAYER: O God, who hast given us bodies to be temples of thy Spirit, help us to control and consecrate body, mind and soul that we may honor and praise thee in all of our ways; through Christ our Lord. Amen.

PUFF-BALLS

High, shrill cries of sea gulls pierced the air. The persistence of excited calls induced a fisherman to row around the corner of an island where he saw a fierce battle stirring. In an inlet surrounded by islands, two tufts of gray were bobbing on blue waters. These puff-balls were the tender brood of sea gulls. Hovering in the air was a large eagle, seeking to capture them

The swift, strong bird of prey was poised for a dive upon the fledglings who were paddling frantically. Sea gulls are not "fighters" and, therefore, no match for an eagle. They are gregarious and readily share with their kind in feeding, training, and guarding of young. But even a large, peace-loving flock was apparently helpless before the fiercest battler of the air.

Instantly the eagle dove with deadly aim at its tender victims. Then an amazing thing occurred. The alert sea gulls swooped at great risk to themselves into the path of the eagle, and in quick succession diverted the aim and deflected the thrust. Attacks were repeated from many angles. The battler was confused. Not only the parent gulls but each member of the flock regarded itself expendable

4

and took its turn unreservedly in this ferocious battle, thus
saving the little puff-balls. Eventually the harassed eagle
flew away.

The beautiful tranquility of the wilderness scene had been
interrupted by a conflict between the strong and the weak.
It was representative of a ruthless and competitive struggle
in the world of man. There have been those in every age
who have built their entire philosophy of life upon the "cruel
struggle" phase of nature and have unfortunately maintained
it to be basic to existence with fellow man. They seek to
justify self-centeredness, exploitation of other humans, and
a heartless attitude toward the underprivileged by what a
wolf does to a deer or a jaguar to a lamb.

Christ challenged such an interpretation of life, chained
to the crude drives of nature. Nature is not a god but God's.
Life was not meant to be lived downward but upward. The
elemental and primitive forces of nature were not to be
masters but servants of human nature. Jesus knew the
storms and conflicts of nature as well as the Roman oppres-
sor's heel, the cruel words of the self-righteous, and the
moan of the hungry and the sick. But he also knew the
capacities of man and the self-giving nature of the Father.

For Jesus the principle of self-denial was not restricted
to heroes and martyrs. "For whoever would save his life
will lose it; and whoever loses his life for my sake and the
gospel's will save it." The law of self-denial is, in fact,
written into everything a man may pursue whether pagan
or Christian. If he wants something badly enough, he will
pay any price for it. But the man who wants to be self-

centered must pay the cost of losing the life of friendship, love, joy, and fellowship. He may let his desires crash-dive upon that which he covets, but the spirit and life are crushed in the talons of lust, greed, and power. We must select that for which we want to live.

As Christ lost his life in a saving ministry among men, an abiding joy was evident. Suffering was not an ordeal inflicted against his will. He accepted this mission from God in the confidence that in self-giving love and in obedience he was expressing the rapture, goodness, and fullness of life as in no other manner. When the world no longer revolves around our own little interests, comforts, and pleasures, and we forget ourselves in him, a new freedom of life becomes ours. What peace to be relieved of worshipping one's own ego! What a joy to be used of God! What a thrill to hazard a swoop into the danger zones of living for the sake of others and to divert the aim of evil from the innocent and helpless. "Remember our Lord Jesus Christ, who though rich for our sakes became poor that we through his poverty might become rich" (2 Cor. 8:9).

❧   ❧   ❧

Whoever would save his life will lose it; and whoever loses his life for my sake and the gospel's will save it (Mark 8:35).

SCRIPTURE READING: John 15:12-17

PRAYER: Gracious God, who in Christ hast given thy life for us, keep us from using strength from thee for purposes which curse our living. We thank thee for all sacrificial lives. Teach us how to bear one another's burdens and so fulfill the law and find the joy of Christ; in his name. Amen.

PRICELESS TREASURES

Minerals, furs, and lumber of the wilderness have demanded their price on the markets of several centuries. However, there is no price tag attached to the serene beauty of a lake and the tranquil majesty of a forest. No commercials interrupt as we gaze at the endless energy of a waterfall or while the bewitching moonlight plays among the rustling birch trees. Who can price the gentle charm of a small, pink wild flower or the shimmering evening stars? The clear, sweet air and the fragrance of the forest are not for sale. The other-worldly splendor of a sunset and the pattern of the spider web, heavy with morning dew, are not quoted on tickertape. No raucous huckster disturbs the singing birds, no persistent sales pitch beckons us to winding trails. The shy deer, half hidden by trees, and the ducks with their zigzagging brood refuse to charge admission. Anyone may become composed and each one may be blessed provided he seeks to carry away a treasure in the heart and not in the hand. Rapture in the wonder and rhythm of life and ecstasy in God's artistry demonstrate that priceless treasures are accessible to all and available everywhere.

When we calmly lay aside the market reports and bank deposit books, it is well to continue to estimate values and appraise treasures until a true total balance of our riches is submitted to the eyes of mind and soul. We need not go

down many trails with friends to learn that affection and trust are not purchasable. Health and healing cannot be bought with fortunes. To share a thought and to see a child's delight in comprehension is of immeasurable value. To love and to be loved, to grow and to help grow, to give and to receive are all balancing figures as we audit the accounts of life.

How deeply satisfying it is to walk in the forest where no fences, walls, or boundaries interfere. Standing on a high cliff, you may claim all the land for a vision from the farthest horizon to the tip of your toes. The vast expansiveness of the heavens, the level stretch of the lakes and the undulations of forested hills bring an exhilarating sense of selfhood and of freedom. There are forests in the world where rusting cannon and barbed wire remind of ugly and discordant forces which would crush freedom and the worth of persons. But here under northern stars, in the land of the loons, one utters a prayer of thanksgiving for freedom which is to be cherished "from sea to shining sea." How can freedom be limited to a few? How may it be reserved for a chosen color of skin? The trees seem to whisper: "Remember your fathers who fought, labored, and dreamed in the wilderness, offering treasures that would claim men as brothers."

Are not the gifts of the Spirit of God freest of all? The Apostle Paul sings out the words: "O the depth of the riches and wisdom and knowledge of God! How unsearchable are his judgments and how inscrutable are his ways!" (Rom. 11:33). When we think of his love and forgiveness, his companionship and his strength, one can only wonder:

"Why does God continue to love me like that?" It is a question we should ponder each day. It leads to many enriching insights.

The questions which are actually foremost reveal our absorption with the wrong treasures. "Can God's resources hold out? Will God provide for tomorrow? How much of these lands and possessions will be mine?" It was hardly coincidence that Jesus was on a mountainside when he said: "Therefore I tell you, do not be anxious about your life, what you shall eat and what you shall drink nor about your body what you shall put on. Is not life more than food and the body more than clothing?" (Matt. 6:25). Who could ever forget this lesson of our Lord as he pointed to the flowers of the field which "grow; they neither toil nor spin; yet I tell you, even Solomon in all of his glory was not arrayed like one of these" (Matt. 6:28b-29a). In frantic concern for physical possessions and security, it is possible to miss the priceless treasures, seen and unseen. Above all, is not the Lord of Life standing in our midst?

❀　　❀　　❀

Ho, every one who thirsts, come to the waters; and he who has no money, come, buy and eat! Why do you spend your money for that which is not bread, and your labor for that which does not satisfy? (Isa. 55:1a, 2a).

SCRIPTURE READING: Philippians 4:4-9

PRAYER: Gracious God our Father, who providest abundantly for each of us as if we were thine only child, and yet sharest so plentifully with all that we must praise thee as one family, accept our individual and united thanksgiving for all thy loving-kindness; through Jesus Christ our Lord. Amen.

ELF TRACKS

The summer morning offered brightness and warmth as guests, including children, were walking along the sandy shoreline. Fascinating tracks were found which small animals had left on the sand during the night. Did they belong to a porcupine or a raccoon? A little girl solved the problem when she chirped: "I think I know what they are! They are elf tracks." All were amused and then our thoughts followed further the childlike fancy. These "elf tracks" were a sign of a healthy imagination, an indispensable gift in discerning the art of living.

Elf tracks reflect the awakening sweep of thought, fancy, and wonder in a child's mind. But imagination follows also more realistic tracks which lead thought and faith to new insights. Uncontrolled, imagination may run away with thoughts and emotions until they become lost in a forest of fears and temptations to make cowards and weaklings of us all. Elf tracks may eventually lead to the footprints of devils or of angels.

The American Indian counseled young braves to walk in another's moccasins for two moons before judging his acts or intentions. Such charitable evaluation of the footsteps of another can be kindled only through the insight of a sympa-

11

thetic imagination. Much injustice and unkindness are occasioned when we do not trace the true nature of the tracks left either by an enemy or a brother. In dealing with members of other races, imagination often has served prejudice, fear, or hatred. Love needs the intelligent and quickening perception of suffering and disappointment, of hopes and capacities in the path of those who have a different color of skin. When we wear another's moccasins the spirit of understanding pursues the tracks of a brother to the place where he lives and learns, works and worships.

Hunters are familiar with the experience of tracking down deer for many miles and then finding that the hounded animal has eluded the dogs by swimming across waters to the refuge of another shore. Imagination has the capacity to cross areas to new freedoms and activities when life seems to have us at bay.

The invalid, the handicapped, and the sick facing their condition prayerfully know something of this saving adventure and activity. Through imagination they are released from the confines of a wheelchair, bed, or room to visit the marvelous and far places of the earth. In fancy they may recall vividly the past, join it with today, and walk into tomorrow. Those involved in the drudgery of daily duty find relief by imaginatively associating their lives with the joy of a family, the fellowship of the church, and with interesting leisure hours.

Christ set a child in the midst of men and women to illustrate the importance of using our imagination in finding the life of God's kingdom. He appealed through every gateway

of mind and soul with picturesque language and vividness
of example. The Bible itself cannot be understood when
read like a creed or formula. Its sentences and chapters
trace the footprints of the mercy and love of God that lead
to shores where life is free, abundant, and joyous.

Sometimes in walking on a sandy shore, one finds the
tracks of a wild goose running in one direction and then
ending abruptly. Frightened by something, it took to the
air. Imagination can give wings to plodding faith. It teaches
faith to look at that which is unseen and upon that which is
not yet. Thus the tracks of spacecraft were first seen on
blueprint paper, and what a boy or girl may become was
first conceived in some heart. Similarly the eye of imagination avoids the experience of evil by foreseeing the consequences. A hard battle may be endured if we can see
what is at stake. When imagination is dedicated to faith it
can say: "Now I know in part; then I shall understand fully
even as I have been fully understood" (2 Cor. 13:12b). Its
wings keep us from being earthbound and assure us that an
Eternal Presence which walked this earth long ago walks
also beside us.

✿   ✿   ✿

*"Truly, I say to you, unless you turn and become like children,
you will never enter the kingdom of heaven"* (Matt. 18:3).

SCRIPTURE READING: Isaiah 35:1-4

PRAYER: O God our Father, who hast bound us together in one
great family to love one another, to enjoy thy creation, and to
find our life in thee, grant us such insight and fellow-feeling that
we may witness to the wonder of thy ways and may be known as
thy children; through Jesus Christ our Lord. Amen.

SILENCE

When the dawn rolls out of coral clouds over the sleepy forest and watery surfaces, it is amazing that something so tremendous and colorful can happen without a sound. No thunderclap, no roaring wind, no trumpet! A new day is being born and it has not yet made its first cry of awakening. While standing in the shimmering dew, one is aware that something mysterious and awesome is happening. This is more than an awakening of the world around us.

14

It is a light from outside the earth which opens eyes, an infinite power from the beyond which causes stirring, a touch of divine intimacy which assures every living thing that it is good to be alive.

Silence to be meaningful must be felt in relation to the Creator and his creation. Otherwise it may become only a time for self-absorption, self-pity, or despair. The silence of the sphinx is maddening, but man made the sphinx. When the Psalmist recalls, "Be still and know that I am God," he knows an overwhelming silence which communicates with his mind and soul and conscience. In such stillness we, too, know the silence of eternity, bounding all the little silences of time.

Unthinking ones regard silence as inactivity. Yet who has heard the flower unfold, the sap flow, the star shine, or the snow fall? Who can hear a thought? Silence introduces us to the area of activities which are essential though unheralded. In the stillness we may sit down, and then walk around ourselves to take a good look at what we are. In the silence our muddled thoughts can settle and clear. As we cease our rushing, fretting, and fuming, and wait patiently upon God, we know ourselves as under his scrutiny. We hear the murmur of an eternal Spirit searching our hearts and trying our ways. We stop being moral ventriloquists. Instead of blaming others we see our own sins and the need of forgiveness. We ask for the "still dews of quietness till all our strivings cease," and then we are ready to receive. The still small voice has a right to be heard and to speak of the dimensions of life in the kingdom of God.

When we approach silence reverently, intimate voices announce precious gifts awaiting us. Strength for the body, composure for the mind, and the renewal of the spirit are offered to the contrite and the trusting. To know the deep stillness of a lake, to revel in the mysterious quietness of a forest, to rejoice in the silence on a hilltop, is to catch some of the facets of God's restoring mercies. Healing, perspective, renewal—these will evade us until we learn to let go of our self-sufficiency and pride. In the presence of him who has ordained the vibrating silence of the night and the revealing stillness of the day, we know the restoring love of Christ. Silence is alive with joy and confidence when we are privileged to confess the beauty of his peace.

* * *

And he said to them, "Come away by yourselves to a lonely place, and rest a while" (Mark 6:31).

SCRIPTURE READING: 1 Kings 19:9-12

PRAYER: Eternal God our Father, who art the Creator of the seen and unseen world around us, quiet our spirits, open our ears and make us hear the things which are good for our souls. We adore thee for every evidence of thy nearness. We praise thee for thy voice in the stillness to which we may listen amid the noise of selfish strife; through Christ our Lord. Amen.

WINDS OF CHANCE

On a woodland path lay an empty nest with two small, lifeless casualties beside it. One tiny survivor, lying on soft ferns, opened its beak wider than its body as it waited for the excited mother bird to bring a worm. The storm of the previous night had torn the nest from the custody of the boughs.

Our companions mused about the circumstances and fate which met the nest and its occupants. What caused that nest to fall and left others intact? Were suspension strands missing? Was it the fault of the nest-weavers, of the wind, or was it an accident?

Our conversation touched upon tragic circumstances of mutual friends. Death, war, accidents, and sickness had left them with the sorrow of "fallen nests" and with unanswered questions. Was their life determined by an impersonal, heartless force? Is the world at times out of God's control?

Every great religion has wrestled with these problems. Some have committed life to the reincarnation of Karma, and others have resigned themselves to a destiny like Kismet. The Fates have been blamed by ancients and moderns

17

for dooming life to a chaotic course. Some self-righteous and fortunate adherents have assumed that the misfortunes of others are a retribution for sins.

On the morning after the bird's nest was dislodged, our boys called from the pier: "Our boat is gone!" Alarming words for island-dwellers! We were fortunate to have our canoe with which to retrieve the boat, found drifting in a hidden bay several miles away. The Bible pictures life honestly with all of its dangers, doubts, and unpredictables. The innocent were not spared, and the prosperity of the wicked evoked moving prayers from the devout. But its men and women who walked by faith never accepted life as being in the grip of a blind, inevitable fate, and they refused to resign themselves to the currents of a capricious chance.

On the contrary, they regarded themselves as accountable before God, regardless of the incalculable factors in life. The stories of man's earliest insight are an accounting in a moral order: "But the Lord God called to the man [Adam] and said to him, 'Where are you?' " "The Lord said to Cain, 'Where is Abel your brother?' " When Moses asked Aaron how the people got the golden calf as an idol, Moses refused to accept the mechanistic and superstitious explanation of his brother, "I threw it [the gold] into the fire, and there came out this calf" (Ex. 32:24). God's fires and gold do not function like that. Man is neither a plaything nor a victim, drifting without excuse. "If God is for us, who is against us?" (Rom. 8:31b). Whether any experience or incident is good or evil depends upon the manner in which it is used or dedicated.

The man of faith reckons with two definite things. First, he knows that he enjoys a God-given freedom through which he may decide how to respond to whatever confronts him. Secondly, he trusts a divine providence which guides and wills good in all events and forces. The unexpected and the uncontrollable are not the basic or final things with which to reckon.

Only a foolhardy canoeist would tempt the law of cause and effect by paddling too close to the brink of a waterfall. God's providence does not rule out his judgment. "For they sow the wind, and they shall reap the whirlwind" (Hos. 8:7a). But it does not follow that all misfortune or even good fortune is merited. Jesus gave a sharp answer to some proud questioners when he said: "Do you think that these Galileans [upon whom a tower fell] were worse sinners than all the other Galileans, because they suffered thus? I tell you, No!" (Luke 13:2-3a). The living ones were requested to repent and to humble themselves for fruitful living because all are recipients of God's grace.

Life, then, is not drifting flotsam. Man has the capacity to entrust his fate and destiny to the God and Father of our Lord Jesus Christ. He may rebuild a "nest," retrieve a boat, portage around a waterfall, choose the currents, and take his chances as he trusts God. For him there is an "out-of-bounds" when life is interpreted cynically without God. He believes that life is "within bounds" of God's sovereignty. He lives "beyond the bounds" as he links what happens in this world with the victory and promises of life to come.

For the Lord our God, the Almighty, reigns (Rev. 19:6b).

SCRIPTURE READING: Luke 13:1-9

PRAYER: Eternal God, who art our Father in good and evil days, we thank thee that thou dost make the heavens and the earth to sustain our life. The farthest sweep of our thoughts finds thee present. The deepest love knows thy Spirit. The greatest need draws thee near. Teach us so to use life's gifts and to respond to all of its conditions that all things may work together for good in the name of thy love that is in Jesus Christ our Lord. Amen.

BEAUTY AFTER THE RAIN

The fragile, pale-blue forget-me-not at our feet, as we alighted from the boat, nodded in accord with our thought that God touches even the isolated places of earth with loveliness. On mountain and plain, in forest and waters, everywhere, majestically and minutely, the divine Artist leaves his signature. This lone flower seemed to extend to us a sacramental invitation to beauty.

A long-awaited rain had adorned branches and blades with precious, glistening drops. The soft duff kept our steps from disturbing the magic setting. We were delighted to find delicate white Indian pipes pushing up through the brown forest carpet. A sweet scent of pine and of aromatic rotting wood hovered around us like incense. Here and there, where boughs had left openings, we saw patches of

azure sky like the subdued light of cathedral windows. We walked a while in this marvelous display which lent itself to every mood. Then in a higher open area we saw granite boulders with pink and gray streaks, bearing their own distinctive beauty. One boulder in the shade wore tall ferns like an Indian headdress. Another in the light carried the lacery of gray-green caribou moss and in the deeper cupped crevices held medallions of darker green moss. On the ground a few stalks of pearly everlasting waved shyly at us. The view of the lake through the trees, the soughing of the unseen wind, the soaring hawk, the diving loon, the lapping of the waves among lilies touched our hearts with joy akin to pain. Rare is the thing God has made upon which he has left no touch of beauty.

We cannot grasp all the wonder of beauty. Its meaning is always eluding us and yet does something to us, leaving us different than before. It speaks to everyone with a silent, winsome persuasion, asking that we look to God to whom all beauty belongs. Beauty becomes a graven image when it is made an object of adoration. Like a sacrament, beauty points beyond itself to him who "has made everything beautiful in its time; also he has put eternity into man's mind" (Eccl. 3:11). It would invite us into the presence of him whose hand and eye planned the sublime loveliness and majestic glory in which we delight.

Beauty dare not become a substitute for truth or goodness. Jesus freed beauty for all realms of life. What he saw in the gentle glory of the lilies of the field, he saw immeasurably more in the faces of children and in the hearts of those who longed that ugly sin might be forgiven. Slums of the city and depravity of man's soul are not in the plan of God. Rather than an escape from life, beauty is a part of the relationships of his children as surely as splendor is arrayed in a wild flower. Men and women were made to clothe themselves not only in Solomon's kind of glory but also in the grace of God's moral and spiritual beauty.

In Christ the all-lovely we have as in none other the beauty of love, righteousness, and truth. Sin adorns itself in beauty to disguise its evil and harmful nature. It ravishes and prostitutes the lovely things for selfish purposes. Christ, on the other hand, came to reveal the gifts of God's love which would restore the inner perspective of man, the quality and dimension of the lovely in our lives. True beauty is where God's Spirit meets a life and where that life responds like a frail flower to the sun. When this "beauty of the Lord our God" is upon us, then the splendor of love, the colors of righteousness, and the glory of brotherhood blend with the beauty of earth and sky and sea.

✿　　✿　　✿

He has made everything beautiful in its time; also he has put eternity into man's mind (Eccl. 3:11).

SCRIPTURE READING: Psalm 19:1-10

PRAYER: Eternal God our Father, who hast filled heaven and earth with thy glory, forgive every thought and desire by which our lives are made ugly in the sight of thy love and goodness. With the power that could transform a repulsive cross into a sign of redemption, woo us into obedience and harmony one with another until we know the beauty of thy holiness; through Jesus Christ our Lord. Amen.

DRIFTWOOD

As we glide lazily upon waters of bays and narrows, fishing is sometimes interrupted when the line is snagged by a hidden log or stump. Occasionally the incident has its unexpected reward in the discovery of a well-formed piece of driftwood. There is no particular artistic standard for driftwood. For the alert eye unusual and sometimes grotesque lines make up a shape and design which have appeal.

Some of the wood may have been submerged for more than fifty years. It represents remnants of trunk, bough, stump, or root—good for nothing. They are nature's cast-offs, old pine or cedar buffed smooth against sand or pebbles by the waves and preserved under water for some appreciative eye.

Form and design vary with the species of wood and grain of the tree. The pieces of knot and their rings or the trunk trays, in contrast to the fantastic root formations, serve to delight the finder. Imagination may run freely as pieces are identified or interpreted. Many fragments of worthless, waterlogged northland pine have found their place as a decoration in some lovely home.

Driftwood reminds us that not all values can be measured in dollars or by conventional standards. If efficiency and financial returns are the only measure of worth, then life has no room for unusual and intrinsic values seen by the imagination. Some things cannot be hurried, nor can they be turned out by a lathe. They refuse to fit into accepted forms. Impressive is the fact that driftwood, though a cast-off, has its use. Not merely is it a camouflage and hiding place for fish in the water; its value for the delight of the eye of man is priceless.

The New Testament is filled with incidents when worthless pieces of human driftwood were found by the Master. Others saw these fragments in the sea of humanity and called them "outcasts," "sinners," "publicans," "unclean." The searching and evaluating eye of Jesus looked upon these misfits and castoffs of society and recognized their intrinsic worth. One needs to work patiently with driftwood. But blessed is the eye which can discern potentials in human life which are in the "rough" though partially hidden by the muck of sin. Each life must be lifted from its hindering entanglements and out of deteriorating waters. Those who love human driftwood see it in the light of its capacities.

So Jesus lifted one neglected and despised life after another from the murky backwaters and barren shorelines of the communities to which he came. He said to the adulteress, "Go and sin no more." To the despised tax collector, Matthew, he called, "Follow me." To Zacchaeus, the small piece of humanity, he expressed the desire to break bread in his home. The story of the young wasteful son was a difficult one to understand for those who, like the elder brother, kept their eyes only upon the exact figures of ledgers and could not see the expression upon the face of a brother in his father's arms.

Not all driftwood turns out well. That does not detract from the beautiful lives which have been found. How will we find that which is worth so much to a holy and loving God unless we continue to search and then leave the evaluation with him?

❋   ❋   ❋

This my son was dead, and is alive again (Luke 15:24).

SCRIPTURE READING: Luke 15:11-24

PRAYER: Father, save us from forgetting all of thy mercies to us and from being envious of thy mercies to others. Keep us watchful to see something of worth in the lives of our fellowmen; through Christ our Lord. Amen.

TRAILBLAZERS

Some of the northland trails originated centuries ago, connecting village and hunting ground, trading post and waterway. Roads and highways have frequently followed their meandering. A trail is an intriguing invitation to the spirit of adventure. Each trail is different from others. Each has a purpose, linking life with the answer to some need or desire.

Many trails still have the characteristics of their origin and destination. There is a trail through pines a hundred years tall leading to a chain of lakes where voyageurs arrived with canoes freighted with furs in colonial times. Not far away a little stream, emitting subdued laughter, runs alongside a path made famous by loggers harvesting virgin pine out of forest depths. Some trails represent the immediate interests of hunters and fishermen, while others recall the journey of explorers, pioneers, and prospectors for new land and minerals. The crisscross patterns of trails, ranging from the Pilgrim Fathers to the Lewis and Clark Expedition, are symbols of varied interest: Some wanted the goods of the new world and others sought freedom; some looked for plunder among Indians, while others were missionaries seeking to bring good news from God.

At the dawn of man's spiritual pilgrimage, there lived a valiant man who was a pioneer of faith in the unseen and living God. He might have retired comfortably, because many years had already left their mark upon him. Yet one day God's call came to him to leave the familiar and to strike out into a new continent of faith. In wandering from Ur of Chaldea, he disentangled himself from a people and culture enmeshed in crass superstition and brutish ignorance. Through his brave commitment to God's purposes, Abraham opened uncharted territory with a trail for all the world to follow. He became the spiritual father of the Hebrew people and of all who would "walk by faith."

While Abraham displayed human frailties, his face was turned toward God. Pressing forward on the trail despite obstacles, he walked toward goodness when he saw it and turned from sin when he recognized it. With eyes upon distant goals, the movement of his life and its forward stance accented an awareness of the future. No wonder God made a covenant with him! For Abraham the promises of God were a staff with which he beat aside interfering branch and brush to find his way.

We blunder if we regard faith as a fine thing in back of us. It is more than a wonderful story of ancient times. Faith is the conviction that something lies ahead with God. It involves us in new areas and experiences of living seen by the Eternal. Faith also demands a choice between a luxurious Egypt and the promises in Canaan. When Lot made a greedy choice of the rich bottom land near corrupt Sodom, it brought disaster. Abraham lived as a friend of God, no matter where.

How indebted we are to those sensitive and sacrificial spirits who blazed trails of faith and of ministry to lives. The call of God comes also to us in new forms of service. We cannot remain exclusively with the old familiar paths nor are we to "settle down in Haran." The early Christians were first called "followers of the Way." Our faith in the kingdom of God, among us and beyond us, will not permit us to "sit" long but keeps us "on the move." More trailblazers are needed in the world in the name of the Gospel. There are "rough places" which need to be made "smooth," says Isaiah, the prophet. The path toward racial equality can no longer be evaded. All the world is asking for directions to the trail toward peace. Christ bestows a great diversity of gifts upon his followers but summons us to be "one in faith" on his way. "And a highway shall be there and it shall be called the Holy Way" (Isa. 35:8a).

By faith Abraham obeyed when he was called to go out to a place which he was to receive as an inheritance; and he went out, not knowing where he was to go (Heb. 11:8).

SCRIPTURE READING: Genesis 12:1-9

PRAYER: God our Father, who in Jesus Christ art our Way, our Truth, and our Life, grant us faith to follow where we see thee not and to love where many love us not, so that we may find each other on our way with thee. Amen.

THE CACHE

An old settler was reminiscing as he walked around the island with us. We came to a sandy clearing surrounded by birch and spruce about twenty-five feet above the water. He pointed at two large depressions in the ground several feet in depth and said, "This is where the Ojibway Indians buried their cache." This had been a camping place for them on long trips where they left supplies until their return. Most Indian caches served as winter storage for family and tribe near their encampment.

The cache was carefully prepared by digging a round pit about five or six feet deep and approximately three feet in diameter. The rough sand was easily excavated with a flat piece of wood or a portion of a moose horn. Birch bark was used to line the walls, bottom and top, while dried grass was packed around and between the valuable store. The cache usually consisted of dried berries, wild rice, Indian maize, and maple sugar. Separate storage basins were often dug for dried or smoked fish. The most valuable cache would not be touched until springtime when its store of priceless seed corn was planted. The hiding place was camouflaged against animals and enemies by covering the top with poles, earth, small plants, and leaves.

Every civilization has had its barns and bins in which to store for winter needs or against lean years. The account of Joseph's farsighted storage during a seven-year abundance in Egypt is typical of how hunger and plenty have determined the destiny of peoples. It is, however, a fatal mistake for individuals or a society to let the cache which supplies creature comforts become the sole determiner of existence.

Jesus stressed emphatically that the soul of man needs bread and treasure which are not found in granaries or banks. Neither are tangible riches a measure of the worth of a person or a people. The Master of life did not overlook physical needs, nor did he despise riches. But when land, property, gold, and food absorb the main drive of life in a man or woman, such a person is making friends with Mammon and not with the living God. He disclosed that the main purpose of all of our striving is to seek after life in the kingdom. God gives us all things to serve this end.

Can you measure or count what has been stored up for your enrichment and blessings in this world? When you were born a precious cache carefully prepared in home and and heart awaited you. Upon entering a library you behold a great heritage from many ages. Who can appraise in currency the price of *Beethoven's Ninth* or *The Gettysburg Address?* Can anyone estimate the value of the Bible, much less the tears, sacrifice, and courage which went into its creation and preservation?

The man who is "rich in things and poor in soul" is to be pitied. His life, which Christ values above things, becomes a mere cache for a hoard of material possessions which today are and tomorrow are no more. "Lay up for yourselves treasures in heaven where neither moth nor rust consume and where thieves do not break in and steal. For where your treasure is, there will your heart be also." The man whose heart is in stocks and bonds or in pleasure and success has not risen much above the simple savage whose entire interest and effort was bent chiefly in satisfying physical hungers.

The Indians had to guard against those who would take from the cache without consideration of community needs or without having contributed their part to the store. Having been blessed physically and spiritually, are we also a blessing?

Life has been entrusted to us to be invested and not to be buried. Generosity, love, and compassion have their risks and need courage, wisdom, and patience in application. The church calls us to a quality of life in which support of worthy causes is as natural as love and breath itself. No one else can express my gratitude to God for me. No other person can determine how the rich resources of Christian love at my disposal are to be invested so that there may be supplies and seed enough for the growth of the kingdom in church and community. The honest man of faith knows that some day his body also will lie as a small cache in the earth. Woe unto that soul that has not laid hold of treasures which outlast death, for it will pass away like the cache of the Ojibway.

*   *   *

For what does it profit a man, to gain the whole world and forfeit his life? (Mark 8:36).

SCRIPTURE READING: Luke 12:16-21

PRAYER: O God our Father, who satisfiest the hungry soul with good things, let not the wants of our body keep us from the nourishment of our spirit; let not our abundance blind us to the need of our fellow man; let not the blessings of others take from us gratitude; and let not our temporal possessions take from our hearts our love of thee and our hope for life eternal; through Jesus Christ our Lord. Amen.

REFLECTED IMAGES

During fishing time one morning, the sun brought a clear, warm day which seemed to hold its breath. The shrill call of the sea gulls contrasted loudly with the stillness of the liquid glass of the lake. Water spiders danced lightly, and beetles had swift maneuvers. A small leaping fish left corrugating circles. Everything emphasized that we were floating upon a perfect mirror. We admired the precise reflection of birch and pine as well as the shimmering outline of a high bluff leaning from a nearby island. Even the bright-blue heavens were reflected by the waters as if to acknowledge their original source. The panorama held us in a quiet spell.

Suddenly a soft breeze chased little ripples across the water pictures, destroying their ephemeral beauty. The last of the images appeared to race toward our boat. The vanishing loveliness evoked wistful reveries as we recalled that we also are bearers of an image. How awesome that in all of his creation God has chosen only man to reflect his own image. We are not divine even as the placid lake is not the forest and sky it reflects. But like the lake, we may reveal that to which we owe our existence and with which we stand in relationship.

No animal has ever stood enthralled by the colored splendor of a sunset. Its satisfactions are limited to physical comfort and security among its kind. Surely an animal is God's creature, and yet the image of God is not given to it. But man beholding nature, so near and real, feels deep kinship and joy with God the Father who has created all things in the universe.

When the Bible speaks of the wonder of God's image in man's keeping, it tells much about his soul and about God. It reflects a personal relationship in which God entrusts life and freedom to use as we please. We may choose between good and evil. We may think God's thoughts after him and in contemplation may bring together yesterday, today, and tomorrow. In a finite manner we may reflect this divine gift creatively in the arts and in literature, in work and in recreation, in science and in faith, in justice and in love. Man can dream beyond that which now is. He may express attitudes and share possessions and find life mutually enriched and enlarged. In having reverent dominion over all things, he is true to the divine image and finds fulfillment when he dedicates all things to the glory of God.

How marvelous that the trees and flowers, animals and stars have their cycles, rhythms, and paths according to the laws of the Infinite. It remains for a human being, by chance sitting in a boat, or following a trail, or peering through a telescope, to interpret these marvels. After looking within and around himself, man is restless with merely the things he can touch and see. The unique gift from God is the capacity to reckon with the invisible and to interpret life in the light of eternity. This is man's grandeur.

The wind, disturbing the beautiful images upon the water,

makes each of us aware that in us and in every man are rebellious thoughts against God which mar our capacity to reflect his love. Evil motives toward fellow man spoil what God entrusts to all. Man's inhumanity to man is like a sinister storm blowing across the divine image. Our broken relationships with God and man haunt us. Freedom and creativity are shackled in the slavery of guilt and vicious circles. The misery of man is that he disobeys God and finds himself forever yearning for the life which comes only out of obedient love for the Father.

Even rough waters from which the images have been obliterated, reflect the blue of the heavens. Though man's image is marred, he is still a child of God. Christ revealed that no man's image of God was meant to be permanently disfigured or lost. God the Creator continues to love us until in calmness of contrition and faith we come to Him to be restored. Christ is the perfect image of God and therefore the image of the perfect man. He is our hope and joy of living because his life and spirit restore the capacity to reflect anew the love, truth, beauty, and grace of God.

*　*　*

God created man in his own image, in the image of God he created him; male and female he created them (Gen. 1:27).

SCRIPTURE READING: Colossians 3:8-15

PRAYER: Our Father, who art the light of life and love, shine into our hearts and gladden them, illumine our souls and purify them, sharpen our minds and consecrate them, and strengthen our bodies to use them. Keep us from evil and make our faces and hands shine with honor and glory unto thee; through Jesus Christ our Lord. Amen.

THE RIDGE POLE

This was the exciting day when we would search for a strong ridge pole to span the space between the apex walls of the cabin. It would support the round pine rafters leaping toward it from the eaves logs. The strength of the roof and the security of the cabin and occupants would depend upon this ridge pole.

We needed a straight Norway pine twenty-six feet in length. One of the woodsmen who had searched the forest with us found a stately tree meeting all specifications. It stood on a steep slope, and a sharp ax soon notched it to fall in the right direction. Swiftly the saw brought the tall tree crashing to the ground. One of the woodsmen called us, and we received a disappointing verdict. The mighty trunk was imperfect at the core; ants had bored deeply into the dry center. How perfect and attractive it had appeared! Now we had to reject it. Sadly we viewed its length of trunk and branches as it lay there, unfit for the purpose for which it had been chosen. Another tree was selected in its place; its healthy rings of growth numbered ninety-four.

It is a significant day when men or women are chosen for the building of a responsible human relationship. Between the apex of the one life and the other there is always a length of experience, knowledge, and faith that must be spanned. This is true for teacher and pupil, husband and wife, as well as for management and labor, citizen and government. In each structure of life the opposite points in youth and maturity, in loneliness and friendship, in need and resources must be brought together under a common roof of love and understanding. The ridge pole of faith must reach from life to life.

What if there is deception during life's growth and process of selection? Suppose a relationship is evaluated as we did the first tree—by outward appearance only? What if the core of friendship or the bond of good faith is rotten, and termites of evil eat away the moral fiber and spiritual strength of "inward being"? When the center of integrity has been gnawed away there is no strength for "spanning" and "supporting" relationships. All of us have heard of cheating in examinations, unfaithfulness in marriage, padding of expense accounts, goldbricking on jobs, dishonest advertising, graft and rackets in the rooms of daily living. But these corruptions are actually an evidence of what has happened to the hidden center of life and relationships. This moral sickness within the heart is a threat to all that shelters the essential and the sacred in the framework of society.

The vitality and health of one's faith is intimately related to these hidden areas of life. In a prayer of self-searching, the Psalmist says: "Behold, thou desirest truth in the inward being" (Psalm 51:6a). We find it difficult to be honest with our heart. It is too painful to see ourselves as we really are. It is easier to pretend that we are someone different. In some of the Greek plays one character is frequently seen holding an umbrella over another obsessed with evil thoughts so that the gods may not see him. But a life of make-believe does not change our "inward being" nor does it prevent the strain of responsibility from exposing the truth.

It is foolish to lie before the all-knowing God. The woodsmen and we were deceived by the visible form of the Norway pine. "Man looks on the outward appearance, but the Lord looks on the heart" (1 Sam. 16:7b). He is not mocked. In fact, God knows all along what we have been and what we are. And yet, in Christ, he loves us. He has accepted us long before we accepted ourselves. The amazing thing is that he still loves us and wants to help us with his truth at the center of our being.

When we approach God honestly it is a most exciting and hopeful moment. Christ "knew what was in man." He knows the evil motives which may be replaced with a new will; he sees low desires which may be dedicated to creative urges; he knows a wavering character which may have a single purpose. Christ can renew the core of our being so that we may support our part in the structure of sacred relationship and holy fellowship.

*Behold, thou desirest truth in the inward being; therefore teach
me wisdom in my secret heart* (Psalm 51:6).

SCRIPTURE READING: Galatians 6:1-10

PRAYER: Our Father, when we open our hearts to thee we are
ashamed. When we see thy face in Jesus Christ we behold thy
love which forgives, thy mercy which cleanses, and thy kindness
which expects much of us. Fill our hearts with integrity so that
none may look or reach to us in vain and each may stand in the
strength of Christ our Lord. Amen.

WONDERS IN MINIATURE

We were peering through binoculars while sitting on the rocky surface of a high bluff. Distant islands, the far-reaching waters, the drifting white clouds, the vast forest-land all seemed to accentuate the fact that the greatness of creation was passing by. Then we laid down the glass on the ledge beside us and began to marvel anew. Here stood a tiny, red lichen flower, unnoticed while we looked upon the expansive grandeur before us. The intricate and delicate pattern of the lichen, known as caribou moss, was a foil for the floral gem. The minute blossoms were but half as large as a small ant. The ant paused, waved its antenna-like antlers as if to sound direction, and then pulled an insect several times its own size toward its hill-home. Farther down on a path, diminutive flowers and shiny leaves of the pipsissewa clung like a sweet corsage against the breast of the earth. Beneath tall balsams and spruce stood a miniature forest of ground pine. These little "trees" attained the stature of five or six inches within fifteen to twenty years. The trill of tiny tree toads and the chirp of crickets emphasized unmistakably the presence of a world in miniature.

We are obsessed with bigness today. Even the power from the infinitesimal world of the atom is used to explore the big worlds in outer space. Great numbers and vastness have overwhelmed many with a sick feeling of insignificance. We have forgotten that bigger cities and bigger institutions do not necessarily produce better people.

We must look not at stars alone but also at fireflies, and we need to remember that God gives light to the infinitely small as well as to the infinitely great. His divine care reaches far and near—as near as a dewdrop, a ladybug or a forget-me-not. The wonders in miniature also disclose God's patient providence and wisdom.

One day Jesus marveled at the tiny mustard seed which may grow into a larger shrub. His disciples were frequently intimidated by the great number of Jewish opponents and by the parade of Roman armies. Their own witness seemed negligible. Now the Master reassured them that tiny beginnings can bring results of magnitude. This is the history of Christianity in many nations and is descriptive of the manner in which God's Spirit still works today. A small child asking questions, a humble home with intelligent love, young people discussing vital problems, a fearless minority contending for truth, one man standing with God—all can grow into "the biggest of shrubs."

Ecologists have an interesting account of how the large
and small plants, shrubs, and trees are interdependent. Each
needs the other in the process of life and decay in order to
propagate, fertilize, and grow. There is also a similar balance in the animal kingdom and between the life of plant
and animal. Even the largest is dependent upon the smallest.

In our human relationships we frequently overlook the
importance and the determining quality of small things. One
word of encouragement, a gesture of courtesy, an attitude
of appreciation, can be like a tiny good seed. One sign of
surrender to evil or one look of assurance in temptation may
be the difference between succumbing and overcoming.

How astounding that "whoever gives to one of these little
ones even a cup of cold water" can be eternally significant
in the judgment of Christ. A gracious spirit may set the
pace for a family circle. The magnanimous attitude may
result in multiplication of forgiveness. Little kindnesses can
bring sweetness where a sour spirit prevails. One loving
heart may become a daybreak among the loveless. Look
and bow your head to see God's wonders in miniature.

* * *

*He who is faithful in a very little is faithful also in much, and he
who is dishonest in a very little is dishonest also in much* (Luke
16:10).

SCRIPTURE READING: Mark 4:30-32

PRAYER: Eternal God our Father, who didst come unto us as a
little babe in a mother's arms to become thy answer to the great
need in every human heart, make us receptive to the gentle as
well as to the powerful forces through which thy Gospel of redemption is brought to all men. Help us to nurture every small
beginning and every worthy growth in thy name. Amen.

SKYLINES IN THE NIGHT

Our family had visited some friends living on an island three miles from our cabin. The moon was almost full that night, and we had stayed until a late hour in the confidence that our way on the lake would be illuminated by its gentle beams. Our path wound around dozens of islands, through narrows, and past dangerous rocks hidden in the shallows.

We were on a wide expanse of the lake when the unexpected occurred. Great clouds moved up swiftly and swallowed the moon. Water and shoreline swam into darkness. We could no longer find a shimmering path, nor could we be sure where lay the depths to carry us safely. Uneasiness crept upon us.

The young skipper of our craft sensed our anxiety and called, "Don't worry, I am following the skyline; it will mark the way." Many vacations had made the wilderness forms and lines familiar. We knew the outlines near at hand. He knew also the distant black tips and undulations of hills, valleys, and bluffs silhouetted faintly against the lighter night sky.

46

Soon we were all joining in the deciphering game. Were there two or three hill tops beyond the next island? Was that large tree there in the daytime? How far from the narrows, cutting the forest outlines, was the flat rock with the buoy? One more ominous expanse of water met us and then we rounded Tomahawk Island. Seldom has a light shining from a cabin cheered us more; we were safely home.

How frequently our calculations and expectations in life go amiss. What we had relied upon has changed, and what gave us a sense of direction has been removed. A cloud of sorrow may hide the light of faith. Financial reverses may darken the future, and a betrayal of trust is like a shadow falling upon a happy path. Physical illness or an unforeseen turn in events may obscure our destiny. We become dismayed with altered patterns when values and guides that stood next to us are gone.

When the immediate events and experiences do not give us direction and when wisdom and judgment which were near at hand disappear into the night, it is good to lift up our eyes. We need to look at the skylines of the Christian hope with its long-range goals. We must search for meaning that outreaches the immediate dark hour. We are wise if we look for the long chain of markers etched against God's heavens and turn to the Gospel of our Lord by which we find the way. Much as we would like, we cannot live undisturbed on immediate interpretations and rewards of life; nor can we continue with only distant visions and hopes. The day-by-day duties and devotion are important, like landmarks; the long-range dreams and hopes are like the skyline, and both are needed.

It is easy to become so absorbed with the daily tasks that one seldom asks what life is about. What does my heart treasure? In what direction am I going? What would I do if what I am now enjoying were removed or were changed radically? Faith in God is a continuing trust and a view by which everything else must and can be steered, even in the night.

❋   ❋   ❋

Let us also lay aside every weight, and sin which clings so closely, and let us run with perseverance the race that is set before us, looking to Jesus the pioneer and perfecter of our faith (Heb. 12:1b-2a).

SCRIPTURE READING: Romans 5:1-5

PRAYER: Everlasting God, our Father, who hast made our feet to walk this earth, grant that our hearts may live in the life of thy kingdom. Help us to lay hold of the things which are not seen but are eternal, and save us from living only for the things which are seen. We would hope in thee in all our ways; through Christ our Lord. Amen.

SCARS

If all the trees bearing outward and inward scars were hewn down, the forests would be pitifully thin. Scars are found on young saplings and on towering giants. Some of the scars are clearly perceptible, and others have been healed over and are quietly guarded within.

There are scars on some of the pine which result from a severe gash caused by a falling tree or the terrible, slithering rip of lightning. Sometimes a portion of bark is eaten away by deer, porcupine, or beaver. The hand of man may have pruned or ruined; a disease may have ravished; a wild growth may have left its mark.

It is amazing how latent powers rally to bring healing growth to damaged areas. Sometimes the wound would have healed better had an experienced hand removed a stub or a fragment of dead wood. In most instances the trees are able to grow to full stature carrying their scars like medals received for brave battle.

Few lives are spared scars from the conflict of life. We need to be charitable with one another because not all scars are borne on the face or body. The mind and personality

also receive their marks of battle; character and soul carry scars as well.

To be afraid of scars is to fear pain and injury involved in the risk and peril of living. A normal attitude of faith regards injury and suffering as incidental to growth and attainment, through love, sacrifice, and service. There are, of course, important differences in the nature of scars. They may be marks of foolish indulgence, of abuse of the body, of evil ways, of broken relations with God and fellowman. They are like the mark which Cain received. These disfigurations are evidences of open and secret consequences of sin and guilt.

Thank God there are also scars which are received because men and women are courageous in the struggle of faith. These are the unavoidable consequences of doing good. Scars are often received when someone exposes himself to danger or hardship for the sake of someone whom he loves. Obedience to a heart of compassion, to larger loyalties and to the will of God can bring scars. These may be worn with honor in God's kingdom.

❋ ❋ ❋

I bear on my body the marks of Jesus (Gal. 6:17).

SCRIPTURE READING: Matthew 27:27-31

PRAYER: O God, who didst not spare thine own Son from death on the tree but gavest him up for us all, we thank thee for the brave men and women who suffered innocently and by choice for the sake of thy kingdom. Grant us strength, healing, and courage to endure hardship as good soldiers of our Lord Jesus Christ. Amen.

A PSALM OF NATURE

It is a curious thing that in the wilderness one may hear a vast company, often unseen, holding forth with solos and choruses of praise. Secluded in favorite choir loft or orchestra pit, these musicians and singers of nature produce antiphonals, chants, and symphonies with infinite variations. These hidden performers present their hymns to the Creator without exhibitionism. Some observers may say that the songs of birds and the chirping of insects can be attributed to calls of mating or flocking, of warning or of delight. Yet such is the beauty and harmony of this unseen chorus that it inspires the spirit of man to rejoice in the invisible God who conceived the score of this "unfinished symphony."

The many combinations of sound and melody gladden day or night. Under the canopy of stars the crickets seem to chirp in rhythm with the beams of light. The frogs render a guttural chant while whippoorwills sing a descant of "his goodwill, his goodwill." In the day as sunlight, color, and sound mingle mysteriously, the bright enchantment of spirit and matter becomes a psalm of praise. In open areas, the skylark, "ethereal minstrel! pilgrim of the sky!" bursts forth with rapturous song. The black-throated blue warbler trills his melody while a lone robin appears like a familiar soloist and sings notes of simple beauty. Lest anyone forgets, the mockingbird repeats a full repertoire of summer joy.

In the background the rolling waves splash against rocks with alternating crescendos of liquid cymbals. Above, the wind plays sweetly an Aeolian harp in the pine boughs. Who can keep a dark mood or a dull temper during this litany of sound and light? Who would close his heart to an exultant spirit? Here is nature, dedicating a psalm of praise to her Creator.

The Psalmist, familiar with Palestinian hills and seas, must have perceived something akin to this wonder when he said, "Let everything that breathes praise the Lord." For him the melodies and overtones of creation were more than a moment of elation out in the "wild." They were an invitation to participate in praise to God who is the Source of all that we enjoy. Ours are even greater gifts than found among the singers in nature; how empty is a soul without exultation in an eternal song of life.

Many sounds are inaudible until one listens intently. Once having heard the whirr of bat wings, the gnawing of a woodworm, the wing-beat of loons, the whizzing of the dragonfly or the drip of resin from a tree, one wonders how many other sounds go unheard. The thankful heart is acutely perceptive of the singing mercies of God. Surely in the cathedral of nature as well as in temple and heart of man, worship is awareness that we are surrounded by invisible choirs singing their hallelujahs to God.

Fortunately, praise to God is not limited to singing or to the sound of an instrument—otherwise many of us would be denied the most important function of life. "Let everything that breathes"—breathes in body and breathes in spirit—"praise the Lord." It is tragic when man, blest with awareness of God and the recipient of his richest provisions, does not use his creative powers in praise. The song of gladness often becomes lost among the tools, the gadgets, the checkbook—the rush of life. Is it worthy of a son or daughter of God when a toothache, a television program, a busy schedule, or an irritation is permitted to stifle the voice of praise?

Some of the most beautiful melodies of the heart have been contributed by those who experienced sorrow, persecution, or sickness. They rejoiced in the everlasting mercy and goodness of God; they knew a risen and living Lord; they forgot themselves and their condition as they acknowledged undeserved love and blessings. Praise was the theme in their devotion to the kingdom. The grace of our Lord exceeds in wonder even the glory of nature. Let us, then, day or night, join the choirs visible and invisible in offering our praise.

❃   ❃   ❃

Let everything that breathes praise the Lord! (Psalm 150:6).

SCRIPTURE READING: Psalm 100; Acts 16:25-28

PRAYER: Father all-glorious, we thank thee for life and its abundance, for mercy which forgives our sins, for loved ones and the warmth of their kindness, for all singers of hope and for thy companionship in Christ. To thee be all honor, glory, and praise. Amen.

FOG

Late in the afternoon on the first day of our canoe trip, rain clouds threatened, and we pitched camp for the night. The rain drops fell leisurely on the warm forest. Each leaf and pine needle released the liquid pellets reluctantly. A lone hermit thrush sang its evening song. The clean air came sweetly into our lungs as sleep enfolded us.

In the gray of morning we broke camp early to keep our schedule. A heavy fog shrouded the lake, and we could not see the opposite shore. Our map and instructions were evidence that others had been at the farther shore and knew the trail leading to a chain of silver lakes. We paddled blindly, counting on each stroke to bring us closer to our destination. Here and there we could see faintly tree tips and then misty rocks as the white bank of fog lowered or lifted.

Suddenly the sun announced the morning. Like an encampment of departing spirits the mists began to move, first from the open waters and then from the bays where the night waited longest. Silently the blanketed spirit-band packed its tents into canoes of rain mist and floated away on currents of the wind. Faintly, then clearly, we saw the beauty of a wilderness trail which had been hidden.

There are times in life when doubts cover our outlook and smother our hopes and plans like a morning fog. Our destinations in terms of goals and attainments are hidden. God seems distant from us. We are like Thomas who would trust only his five senses to assure him of the presence of his Lord.

We cannot postpone living; each of us has a schedule to keep on the way. While doubts may retard us and uncertainty makes us cautious, life must go on. Many a paddle stroke has to be taken in the fog of skepticism. We then do well to rely upon the testimony of the men and women who have known and seen the shorelines of the kingdom of God. Their experiences become maps of faith which we must follow anew in our life. There comes a moment when we must go farther than we can reach and see, and we trust God.

Faith is an essential element for all living; we never outgrow it; each must have his own. The scientist experiments by faith long before he can put a formula on paper. No court could uphold the law if all evidence had to be visible. A house is built upon a contract, but a home is created upon a covenant of faith in each other's love. Prayer is faith that God will answer our heart's cry. The church is a fellowship of imperfect men and women who have faith that God's Spirit calls them to serve Christ. The Christian is confident that God is beyond the immediate fog of doubt, of struggle and of suffering, and has a plan and purpose for us in his kingdom. What a mistake it would be to cut off our adventure of living because we cannot always see everything ahead of us. Morning calls and we must go on until the fog lifts. Then we shall see a trail before us.

* * *

Now faith is the assurance of things hoped for, the conviction of things not seen (Hebrews 11:1).

SCRIPTURE READING: Hebrews 11:1-6

PRAYER: God and Father of our life, broaden and deepen our faith in the pain of doubt, strengthen our convictions at the cost of struggles. Grant us wisdom to walk obediently in all that we see and teach us to trust thee where we cannot see until we come to the knowledge of thy truth and love through faith in our Lord Jesus Christ. Amen.

LITTLE CREATURES

Early in the morning the children called us to come out-side quickly. One large, one medium-sized, and one tiny mouse had fallen into a newly dug hole where we were building. As we peered over the edge they burrowed tan fur and deer-like ears into the sand until only their tails were visible.

Our children were especially concerned about the owner of the smallest tail. We took a long birch pole and placed it into the hole at an angle. First the largest deer-mouse took a peek and then the others stirred and blinked. The next instant the large mouse scurried to the bottom end of the pole and climbed up in rapid, spiral fashion. Then the mite of a mouse imitated the large one and finally the medium-sized prisoner, having waited patiently, followed round and round the pole until it also reached the safe ledge and could scamper beneath a carpet of bunch berries.

We often wondered how the "mouse minds" explained the arrival of the rescuing birch pole. Perhaps they never did, but they lived and rejoiced in the realm of mice because of it. Frequently we would limit God's providence and love to our understanding of it. We exclude the mysterious working of higher laws and powers beyond those which we have tested in laboratories and written into textbooks. Our forefathers knew little or nothing about some elements in God's creation which have become essential to our life, such as the atom, the ocean currents, electric waves, and the wonder drugs. Lack of knowledge about these matters did not nullify either their existence, their potential influence, or God's use of them. Each generation wrestles with the problem whether the science of the day or faith should formulate thinking about God. In a day when the surface of the world was regarded as flat and when the sun was thought to orbit about the earth, Jesus let his faith in God as Father determine basic assumptions about nature, human nature, and the nature of the divine. "Look at the birds of the air: they neither sow nor reap nor gather into barns, and yet your heavenly Father feeds them. Are you not of more value than they?" (Matt. 6:26). Then observing both the good and evil in man, he would have us take our clue from the best and proceeds to the "how much more" of God. "If you, then, who are evil, know how to give good gifts to your children, how much more will your Father who is in heaven give good things to those who ask him?" (Matt. 7:11). God's creatures may be small and limited but his wisdom and providence are infinite and often beyond our comprehension. Faith trusts that this is "our Father's world." Increase in knowledge about the nature and the vastness of creation need not cancel faith. Rather, an adventurous spirit in any realm joins faith in leaping beyond reason and knowledge, trusting that God is also there.

Early one spring we were surprised by visitors in a kitchen drawer in the cabin. Two beady eyes greeted us from a fluffy nest, made from what had once been a ball of string. Furtively the mother mouse looked about and gathered six members of her brood and deposited them by mouth in another corner of the drawer. Again she observed us apprehensively and saw that this was scant security in the presence of the giants watching her. She returned to her family and then left very deliberately over the back of the drawer. Dangling from the underside of the mother were five little mice. But we heard another squeak in the nest. Had one been forgotten? We waited and a little later the mother returned from out-of-doors. She crawled into the nest and emerged swiftly with the sixth of her brood. Adroitly carrying in her mouth a tiny creature with a long tail, she disappeared to a forest refuge.

When our Lord alluded to birds, flowers, and little animals, he revealed an absolute conviction that our heavenly Father cares and provides for every living thing. What we often regard as the "wilderness" is, in fact, an area in which an all-knowing and gracious God, through intricate design and surveillance, provides for everything that has breath. Jesus looked upon the creatures of nature as his friends because they were God's creation. How naturally it followed that God could be counted upon to extend this divine care into every realm of life that he had called into being. "Your Father knows what you need before you ask him"

(Matt. 6:8). It is easy to forget, but isn't your life of more value than a little mouse?

*   *   *

Will he not much more clothe you, O men of little faith? (Matt. 6:30).

SCRIPTURE READING: Matthew 6:25-33

PRAYER: Almighty God our Father, may not thy majesty and power hide thy love for us and may not our weakness and doubt keep us from trusting thy goodness to us and for all mankind. Free us from anxious thoughts about tomorrow. Grant that we may trust thee with our love and service today; through Jesus Christ our Lord. Amen.

AHEAD OF US

Having moored our boat at a wilderness landing, we shouldered our canoe more than a mile and at last, tired and happy, came to our first stream. Our paddles touched white water lilies and spatterdock, smooth jutting granite boulders and blades of cattails. Several portages later, having found a good island camping place, we were conscious that we were guests of the Creator in a setting of breathless beauty.

On one of the small side trips into the forest we found a bed of ferns and a carpet of moss. A few steps farther, a large patch of delicious blueberries was spread before us. We were awed that God had been there ahead of us. It humbled us that divine preparations should have been made for our coming to this wilderness tryst. We began to think of how God anticipates all of our arrivals of time, place, and experience in life.

As we continued our explorations and found an arrowhead, we became mindful that long ago some Indian and his family must have cast their eyes upon the symphony in color as it interplayed with blue sky and cloud-reflecting waters. The forest banks must have stood like a silhouette on the border of this paradise. As he hunted and fished, the Indian was unaware that there were civilizations in other portions of the world. Abundance and security were

elusive as he sought livelihood. But in his primitive faith he trusted the present and learned to hope for sufficiency in the future from the Great Spirit.

Nature has been getting ready for man ever since it awoke from its primeval void. God has been out in front inviting the mind of man to discover and search in this world as well as in outer space. He has placed treasures on hillside and in streams. Precious things are buried in the heart of the earth. Wherever man goes he finds that God meets him with goodly blessings. The Bible confirms that God has faithfully made preparations for man's grand portage across the earth. Here he placed a man of faith, there a noble prophet; his law thundered down a mountainside, and his forgiving mercy flowed as refreshing streams.

This is what makes Christ so amazing; he is timeless and anticipates the yearning and need for redemption of each life and of every age. God's love in Christ touches earth just ahead of us and is as ancient and as new as the heart-beat of humanity. He is always waiting for our steps to catch up with him. Many good things are in readiness for each of us. By faith we are sure that Christ also prepares for us beyond our earthbound existence.

❋   ❋   ❋

For thou dost meet him with goodly blessings (Psalm 21:3).

SCRIPTURE READING: Psalm 23

PRAYER: Gracious God and Father, who art ready to meet us with good things, grant us courageous and expectant hearts as we come to new and unknown experiences in life. We would trust thee to provide for our needs as disciples of thine; through Christ our Lord. Amen.

RIDING WITH THE WAVES

It was a beautiful summer day, and the wind blew its clean breath vigorously across the lake. Whitecaps were racing with puffy white clouds. We used the boat and canoe to transport our guests and family to the mainland shore for some swimming with friends. The wind nudged us playfully as we rode the exhilarating cadence of the waves.

The hour of return came all too soon while the wind had increased its velocity. Rough waters tossed wildly both boat and canoe. Someone suggested tying the canoe to the boat as a measure of safety to lessen the heaving. A rapid and radical development ensued. The ropes which fastened the canoe to the boat prevented the lighter craft from riding with the waves. The canoe was held down when the waves swept higher, and it was soon swamped by the backlash. Fortunately the canoe was unsinkable and the occupants were good swimmers. We had not made much headway, and turned in to the shore at Listening Point. The friendly figure of a wilderness guide was watching us with experienced eyes and came to give a helping hand. He confirmed what we had learned: "Never lash a canoe tightly to a boat in tossing waters; let it ride with the waves."

This principle of good canoeing has its counterpart in our relationship one with another. Parents, leaders, or teachers, for example, are often tempted to tie youth too tightly to their own broader knowledge and experience in the hope of providing help and security. But oversolicitude may inhibit self-confidence and initiative. On the other hand, a dominating approach may nurture conformity and dependency.

The challenge to know oneself as a person with talents and worth, unfolding before God and man, makes life as mysterious as tossing waves. Yet each of us was meant to ride with the waves in his own way. There is a moment in every relationship when the individual's personality and initiative must be given free play. Rather than seek quick perfection, a good teacher will permit the full rhythm of trial and error and of eventual attainment. Instead of continually shielding his pupil against dangers, there is the alternative of permitting him to face uncertainties honestly in the adventure of learning and of living.

We must also be courageous enough to ride the waves of our personal sorrow, pain, or disappointment. We cannot avoid these turbulent moments of the human spirit. Nor dare we try to suppress them within. They must be permitted full movement until they meet the calmness of faith and the strength of God's love.

The disciple Peter wanted to prevent Christ from facing the crest of the waves of opposition and of death during the last weeks of his ministry. This shortsighted counsel for physical security could have capsized the entire moral and spiritual mission of Jesus. Rather than protect himself from the impact of the waves of evil, Christ faced their fullest fury and the length of their sweep and thus was able to reveal the nature and power of the redeeming love of God.

* * *

I know how to be abased and I know how to abound; in any and all circumstances I have learned the secret of facing plenty and hunger . . . I can do all things in him who strengthens me (Phil. 4:12-13).

SCRIPTURE READING: 2 Timothy 2:1-13

PRAYER: Father, who at all times watchest over all thy children, give us courage to face difficulties with strength, hardships with endurance, ignorance with wisdom, and doubts with faith. Give us grace to mature in all things until we reveal the spirit that was in Christ. Amen.

INDIAN PAINTINGS

The songs that an Indian mother cooed over her papoose and the vows which young men and maidens spoke when the crocuses bloomed and wild geese returned have been carried away forever by the west wind. Under starry skies or by lighted fires, while wolves howled in the distance, braves would recount stories of heroism, and wise ones would tell about the Great Spirit inhabiting the world around them. No library or museum was there to immortalize their precious heritage. Yet the essential things in life were communicated through voice and design in family and tribe.

Some of the rare evidences of the more permanent means of communication among the early Indians are the creations of poet-artists, preserved on the face of high perpendicular cliffs at the edge of the waters of Crooked Lake, Lac La Croix and North Hegman Lake. These painted Indian symbols are surrounded by a mystery of authorship and age. As the canoe rounds the bays one is hushed by these simple creations on great walls. Here had been man, communicating not like the animals and birds but to future generations what was in his mind and soul.

Man has come a long way from those early drawings on the rock walls, painted perhaps with a mixture of muskellunge oil, iron oxide, berry juice, or crushed clays. They are no comparison to present-day printing, radio, television, or art. We might well ask, however, whether with the efficiency and complexity of our media of communication we have also developed our integrity of mind and heart. The clear, searching admonition of Jesus: "Let what you say be simply 'Yes' or 'No'" (Matt. 5:37) is still essential if we would inspire confidence and speak with authority among peoples of all races, classes, and conditions.

The excellence of our modern means of communication must not silence the fundamental question: "Have we anything to say to each other and to the world? Is it vital to life? Have we the kind of message that will blend as naturally and consistently with God's creation and purpose as those simple, colored paintings on granite walls blend with the lapping waters, whispering trees, and blue skies?"

It is not the medium and the technique alone but that which we would say to each other which is of primary importance. Forgetting this, we may write, sketch, or speak endlessly about new styles, modern shops, good investments, better schools, luxurious clubs, larger granaries, or even stately churches and miss communicating that life which outlasts these material things by which we are so absorbed. Certainly we need more than the voicing and dramatizing of primitive hungers and drives. Men and women are waiting for the kind of bread which feeds the soul. They are looking for new creations and designs of the Spirit of God which replace prejudice with understanding, lies with truth, corruption with justice, and hate with love. Jeremiah hears God describing it: "I will put my law within them and I will write it upon their hearts and I will be their God and they shall be my people" (Jer. 31:11). Modern media have not changed these elemental requirements in spite of a barrage of the superficial and the false upon eyes and ears.

The Christian Gospel gives us a word from God in the language of every soul. It is a word that God spoke through Christ and that he continues to speak to us and to our times. This portrait of the saving love of God is the burden of the preaching and teaching of the Christian church. The early Christians etched familiar signs of the fish and the cross in catacombs and on street walls by which to identify and guide each other. Above all, they were living witnesses, "letters of recommendation, written on hearts, to be known and read by all men."

It is really not so far from the childlike Indian paintings about hunting, seasons, game, and the heavens to the crayon drawings of our own children. But how will our children go on to draw in real life, with color and perspective, their understanding and experience of the things by which a Christian lives? Dictators know that there need be only one generation without faith and a pagan ideology may be implanted for generations. Even in a democracy, the good does not automatically communicate itself. Learning and speaking about faith remain as personal a matter as Indian

paintings—as essential as that which the Indians did not write on walls but dramatized nobly and tenderly for each other in their family and tribe.

*   *   *

You yourselves are our letter of recommendation written on your hearts, to be known and read by all men (2 Cor. 3:2).

SCRIPTURE READING: Romans 10:12-17

PRAYER: Our Father, we thank thee for our Christian homes through which thy mercy and lovingkindness first came to us. We are grateful for teachers and friends who illumined thy truths and shared thy Spirit. We praise thee for thy Spirit's guidance and teaching through Bible and prayer, through sacrament and symbol. Grant that we may express our gratitude for all mercies received by becoming faithful witnesses in all our ways, to thy honor and glory. Amen.

A LANDING PLACE

Excitement is high when we make our initial seasonal approach to the island. Formerly we resorted to the primitive maneuver of stepping upon a rock or log to reach the land. Then as soon as possible we replaced the large dock posts which wind-driven ice floes had carried away. Even when the posts and planks were restored, landing was precarious and the moored boat had little protection during storms.

When a long dock of pine logs was built and its crib-like design was filled with tons of rock, it was like a thirty-foot-long bridge of hospitality from shore to boat. It became a permanent and pleasant aid to alighting and for secure mooring.

How priceless are the friends who are a landing place for mind and heart and soul. Like a dock reaching beyond the shallow and slippery beginnings of the shoreline, they extend trust, and we follow in devotion; they link us with good companionship, and we find a wealth of wholesome incentives; they introduce us to good books, music, and recreation, and our talents are called to respond with their best.

The experience of stepping from childhood to youth is emotionally bewildering. The surge of new powers through physiological changes is frequently perplexing. Our minds, too, may be perturbed by vexing questions. We then seem strange to ourselves and find our companions likewise unfathomable. It is in such quandaries that an understanding friend is as a steadying arm which secures a tossed craft to a place where one may walk with confidence.

Fortunate is that child who has parents that awaken curiosity in the wonders of the surrounding world and extend a guiding hand for the first step with an assuring word for unfolding mysteries. Students identify quickly the teacher who encourages an inquiring mind to touch the shores of a new truth or activity. Those who limit teaching to imparting of impersonal facts offer no inducement to step into new realms of thought and relationship. It is a privilege to be greeted by those capable of unfolding life's meaning. They meet us where we are, reach for our response and give solid footing to curiosity and energy in the venture of learning.

Young John Mark was floundering through inexperience and discouragement after deserting an important mission. Paul no longer had confidence in him. Then Barnabas extended steadying encouragement, and John Mark landed on the good footing of a new beginning. We know the trust was justified when we read the Gospel named after him. Lydia, a wealthy business woman, seller of fine cloth, offered the gracious hospitality of her home to Paul and to new Christians so that the church might establish a beachhead in Philippi. Paul himself set the entire European landing mission into motion when he recognized that the Gospel of his Lord was meant for every shore and every continent.

Unforgettable is the experience of arriving at a dock in the night and hearing the greeting of a loved one though no one can be seen. The pier becomes an extension of everything that is precious, and it meets us with every reason for wanting to make a landing. From the emergence of the first glimmer of faith in the soul of man, the deepest problems of life have concerned themselves with the questions: Who meets us in the unseen? Will God speak to us? Is life worth coming home for? Is there meaning beyond the darkness? Christians are convinced that God has come to meet them in Jesus Christ as in none other. He unveiled the splendor of God not by withdrawing from sinful men but by letting lowly mercy and saving love reach to the outcast, the sinful, and the needy. He is the only true Mediator between the Father and us. He is the fulfillment of all steps of faith and the answer to all reaching toward the shore of the kingdom of God. We may moor our little ship of faith to this Dock even when earthly sight fades into darkness.

❊   ❊   ❊

And he brought him to Jesus (John 1:42).

SCRIPTURE READING: Hebrews 4:14-16

PRAYER: Father, we thank thee for all who have inspired us with their faith in thee, who have led us with knowledge from thee and who have wooed us from things unworthy with a love for thee. Bestow upon us the grace to forgive those who have hurt us and to help those who need us so that thy love for us may be felt and understood by all; through the power of thy Spirit which was incarnate in Jesus Christ our Lord. Amen.

THE LURE OF ISLANDS

Standing on a high point on the wooded mainland south-west of Burntside Lake, you see the rare beauty of some fifteen islands lying like a stately armada in green, waiting for favorable winds while anchored offshore. These islands are among more than one hundred in the lake, so typical of the northland. Do they intrigue because they are reminiscent of some "Treasure Island"? Or is their insular beauty alluring because they are away from humanity and possess untouched wild charms, infrequent on the mainland?

Islands remind us of our selfhood. They reflect the variety of personalities among us and the countless capacities with which each of us is endowed. They intimate that within each individual there is much to be found and explored that is of infinite worth. The crowd belongs to the mainland. To keep our identity we must separate ourselves from the pressures and entanglements of the masses. A community

76

is most vital when it is composed of individuals who know themselves to be precious fragments of humanity. Frequently the standards of the crowd and the opinion of the public are held supreme. Mass appeal often stifles the lone thought or conscience. We need a spiritual "island experience" in which we may withdraw to catch up with the self we ought to be and to face the self we are. Islands lure us to gain a renewed sense of self.

There are times, however, when an island is completely isolated from the mainland by storms or by treacherous ice. Such periods change a wholesome and pleasant existence into dangerous isolation. John Donne wrote the unforgettable lines: "No man is an Iland, intire of it selfe; every man is a peece of the Continent, a part of the maine" (1573-1631). We are linked to the mainland by the very nature of our being, need, and purpose. No one is physically, culturally, intellectually, or spiritually self-sufficient. We are the solitary whom God has set in families. We need to withdraw at times from the many voices among which we cannot hear our own; yet we recall how we have also been blessed and sustained by a great host of all ages as we join in work or play and as we share our worship and dreams.

The story of Robinson Crusoe is an entrancing fancy. But to choose an "island type" of existence even while remaining in the midst of society is essentially selfish. Getting all the benefits you can from a community, then running away without giving anything in return is hazardous, insular living. To seek comforts without bearing the burdens of our fellow man is moral isolationism. To enjoy privileges without remembering those whom God remembers is to cut oneself off from man and God. That is the essence of sin on the island and mainland of living.

There comes a time when we, like Robinson Crusoe, come across the footprints of a man Friday. Life is so involved that we soon meet a man Monday and a man Tuesday and many more. Of greater importance is the search for the man Sunday in our small and great worlds. "For we are members one of another," said the first Christians. They were a fellowship which was aware of a Presence in its midst. Here were new lives and a new way of living together.

The Christian church seeks to help each person discover the Gospel for himself. Christ offers an invitation for all and an appointment with each of us personally. But Christ cannot be kept in one heart alone, nor can we fully find him until we also have come to the mainland of Christian fellowship in faith and love. The kingdom of God embraces the island and mainland—the individual and society—and promises fulfillment to both.

*   *   *

So we though many, are one body in Christ and individually members one of another (Rom. 12:5).

SCRIPTURE READING: Romans 12:1-8

PRAYER: We thank thee, O God, for thy goodness and mercy toward us in Jesus Christ through whom we are united in a fellowship of life and love. Keep us mindful of all who sacrificed and persevered that we might receive the heritage of the Gospel through thy church. Make us sensitive to our brother's need. Form us into good members of the family of faith; through Jesus Christ our Lord. Amen.

BEAUTY WITHIN

The Finnish stone masons knew how to select beautiful granite rocks for the interior of the cabin walls. The pink and gray boulders, streaked and speckled with infinite variations in white and black, contained hidden beauty the untrained eye could not always discern. But the masons would deliberately turn the stones until they ascertained the grain of the rock. Then from many precise blows of a heavy stone hammer, the rocks would usually split in the manner desired. The new scintillating surfaces shone with countless brilliant flecks in a setting of pastel shades. Some possessed rare and intriguing markings of black and green. Only those rocks which disclosed a beauty within were used inside the cabin where their smooth surfaces could delight the eye.

We admired the Finlanders who looked not only at the outward appearance of the rocks but searched for inner beauty. This art of discernment is of even greater value in matters of life and faith. The Apostle Peter points out that there were some builders who failed to see the nature of Christ's life and teaching. "The very stone which the builders rejected has become the head of the corner" (1 Peter 2:7). The builders of the religious life and moral system of that time were almost exclusively interested in external regulations and observances. Jesus took issue with the crucial weakness of religious practices which dealt with the outward forms and which failed to show beauty and loveliness within the heart. The splendor of temple and of ritual was not an adequate substitute for lives which were like beautiful white mausoleums but lifeless within.

When Jesus rejected some applicants for membership in the kingdom of God and accepted others, he shocked many with his selections. The rich young ruler was a good prospect and Jesus loved him, but there was no beauty within—he was loveless. Zacchaeus was hated by many, yet Jesus saw a heart that was charitable and loved God. The eyes of Christ search the core of our living. Are our prayers external recitations like those of the conceited Pharisee, or are they like the inward penitence of the publican? We cannot live by practices and standards which appear outwardly clean but whose inner motives are repulsive. The first-century Christians were called "living stones" in the church which was built by faith in Christ. Only such stones have the quality of "beauty within."

The rocks intended for the cabin did not always split satisfactorily. Some broke into many fragments and others had a crooked grain, resulting in jagged surfaces. The blow of the hammer, instead of revealing hidden beauty, rendered them useless. All of us have known lives which were shattered by misfortune or tragedy. Untouched by adversity, they impressed us favorably and seemed to join well in the structure of living. Then came a blow which exposed the quality of their character and the texture of their faith. The impact of a severe test revealed an inadequate quality of inner strength; therefore they disintegrated.

Some of the most inspiring lives of history have been those that were split wide open by the hammer of God. Such a man was Stephen, a distinguished lay leader and administrator in the church. He also cultivated the gifts of the Spirit within his soul. Then came a fateful day when this brave young man was martyred by those whose hearts were harder than the stones they hurled. His face shone as he prayed for his enemies. A "living stone" like Stephen may turn itself to such an angle of faith that the shattering blow of adversity reveals unsuspected beauty of the spirit of Christ.

The cabin walls which the Finlanders built are singularly attractive. A decorative blending is created by the combined beauty within many stones. So true homes are built where the loveliness and integrity of each member are shared in the family. A lasting fellowship of learning may be established where minds share, beyond formal knowledge and wisdom, an understanding concerning life in the kingdom of God. Churches are built well and become effective when they consist of "living stones" mortared together by the unity and love which are in Jesus Christ. Some interesting words are attributed to Jesus in an old manuscript: "Raise the stone and there thou shalt find me; cleave the wood and there am I." As Christians we need to examine our lives repeatedly from every angle as to whether the grain of conviction penetrates to the center of our being.

*   *   *

And like living stones be yourselves built into a spiritual house, to be a holy priesthood, to offer spiritual sacrifices acceptable to God through Jesus Christ (1 Peter 2:5).

SCRIPTURE READING: 1 Peter 2:4-10

PRAYER: O God our Father, who hast entrusted to us our bodies to be the dwelling of our souls, and hast given us our souls in which the Christ would be our guest, grant that we may prepare ourselves so consistently and thoroughly that at all times we may receive thee unashamed and may accept thy will with joy; to thy honor and glory. Amen.

THE TWISTED PINE

There is a lone, gnarled Norway pine standing on the point of a nearby island which evokes a salute of the spirit as we paddle by. It is much older than the taller, neighboring pines behind it in the forest. The reason for its dwarfed size is to be found in the limited quantity of soil on the rocks where it grows. Roots have nowhere to go but to reach into crevices, and during a period of drought there are no deeper sources of moisture. It must content itself with limited growth. The storms hit this Norway directly from the northwest. The companion trees are not near enough to take the brunt of the wind. The surge of life, resisting wind pressure, has caused the trunk to spiral upward so that the tree has a twisted shape. It is evident that every inch of wood and each needle on the tree is borne proudly because of this relentless battle against the elements with a resourceful pattern of roots in poor and limited soil.

Such a gnarled Norway pine would not be chosen by popular standards as a figure to embellish a coat of arms. Nor is it likely to become for many young people a symbol of a future vocation. The trees that might be chosen to grace a modern escutcheon would be those growing strong and tall rapidly. These would be the symbols of great success, of rapid advancement, of high salaries, of influence with prestige. But the choice of such a conventional design would overlook the greatest ennobling and enriching spirit found in the human heart, characterized by the twisted Norway pine standing dauntlessly upon rough rocks and meager soil. This spirit courageously accepts a call from God to serve and to inspire where there is the greatest challenge in terms of human need, without thought of reward. This noble human quality and approach to life is frequently ignored as eyes turn to the more popular demand for ease and wealth and acclaim.

The fact that those who have accepted a call from God may have to work under difficulty does not dissuade them from sinking their roots into so-called barren areas of human life. By their standard what happens to men, women, and children is more significant than fluctuation of values in stocks, property, and real estate. It is sufficient for them to know that this is where God desires work to be done in the name of love which dignifies and restores life. This revolutionary spirit which prompted Christians to stand in unconventional and dangerous places among humanity, brought healing to lepers, compassion to the mentally sick, mercy to the crippled, care to the aged, education to the ignorant, and opportunities to the dispossessed.

Today this same spirit seeks out the blighted and underprivileged areas of human existence. It accounts for brave ones facing death-dealing diseases, searching for cures; for social workers carrying a heavy case load, giving cover to the exposed roots of family life. This is the spirit of nurses caring for the critically ill, of teachers seeking to enlighten

impressionable minds in the midst of crass environment, of clergymen endeavoring to shepherd those who have lost the way of faith. It motivates countless others who in their own way have caught the spirit of him who "came not to be served, but to serve, and to give his life as a ransom for many" (Mark 10:45). Is it not strange that society crucified him on a lonely tree?

Those whose armor for living bears the insignia of the twisted pine furthermore reveal a staying power under great difficulty. They remain beside discouraging and exhausting circumstances because they know that God stays there, too. This again is a spirit which clashes with the image of the large, tall tree symbol with the motto: "I will serve as long as conditions and results are ideal." Those who have staying power in their calling and in their concern for humanity "suffer hardship as a good soldier of the Lord Jesus Christ." Many will not see them. Others, seeing them, will ignore or ridicule their high calling. But when you look at them, silhouetted against the sky, they stand as inspiring sentinels of God.

❖   ❖   ❖

"The Spirit of the Lord is upon me, because he has anointed me to preach good news to the poor . . ." (Luke 4:18a).

SCRIPTURE READING: Luke 4:18-30

PRAYER: Gracious God who art found among all conditions of men, we thank thee for all who in thy compassion and strength have stood among the forgotten, the helpless, and the despised. Grant that we may judge no one by circumstances but in thy love. May our manner of making a living help others to live; through Jesus Christ our Lord. Amen.

THE WELL

Hidden by boughs of birch and spruce stands an old-fashioned hand pump. The water it lifts from the well on the island is clear and cold even on the hottest summer day. Its refreshing stream came as a rich reward for the labor and sweat required to discover the source and dig the well. In four different locations our shovels struck a far-running rock shelf six or more feet beneath the surface. In the fifth excavation we came upon quicksand with all of its sucking and caving characteristics. Then we decided to attempt once more to reach water. Arduous labor had its reward as a clear stream sickered into the hole to an adequate depth.

A pleasant interlude occurred when a friendly and enterprising neighbor arrived from the mainland and extolled the mysteries of "water witching." He grasped a forked willow stick firmly and walked about the area until his "divining rod" bent downward. It indicated water on the site last chosen and also where the stone shelf had prevented further progress.

Water is indispensable to life. One good drink in large quantity on some notable occasion is not sufficient to quench our thirst on succeeding days. No wonder the poet describes the elemental need of the soul with a striking picture: "As the hart longs for flowing streams, so longs my soul for thee, O God. My soul thirsts for God, for the living God" (Psalm 42:1-2).

One day Jesus met a Samaritan woman at the famous Jacob's well. Her character was murky and her interest in religion superficial. She had sipped at this tawdry pleasure and at that shallow relationship with the aftertaste of disillusionment and instability. Jesus sensed her distress and fundamental need, as real as the large, empty jars she had brought to the well in the hot sun. For parched souls he could offer "living water." So satisfying was this refreshing assurance that we are told "many Samaritans believed in Jesus because of this woman's testimony." She found the God who is Spirit and who must be "worshipped in spirit and in truth." Here were waters of "eternal life" from the deep.

The well illustrates that the waters which slake the thirst of our inner being cannot be procured easily. Shallow experiences offer waters that are tepid, polluted, unpalatable. Living communion with God cannot be established in little puddles of self-concern and in casual interest in religion. The difficult and deep digging of repentance and of longing for grace finally "strikes" the living water.

We were never able to validate the interesting "water witching" demonstration. But we know that there are some who attribute special powers to their own "divining rod" in matters of faith. Astrologers make personal claims based on the movements of the impersonal stars. Spiritualists disregard the adequacy of the Spirit of Christ for life in this world. Some religious healers profess fantastic cures and ignore what God does through science and faith working hand in hand. Others would harness streams of God's life to their own dynamos of success and popularity. Jesus did not limit the well of "living water" either to Mount Gerizim or to Jerusalem.

The simple, old-fashioned pump over the well in the forest arbor is reminiscent of days prior to modern power pumps. The Bible is often identified with times and customs of an ancient era. So Jesus is considered as adequate for his day but as obsolete for our era of superb scientific achievements and culture. But the things of time must not be confused with the timeless. Long ago people drew water out of wells with ropes and buckets. Our children will use atomic energy to bring water from the depths. We forget that it is not the pump but the water which is the constant need in each generation. Our methods of studying the Bible may change; we may discover more historical and archeological data; new translations may clarify words and phrases; science may continue to reveal the marvels of the universe. But the hand pumps of the past and the innovations of the present must not deter us today from drinking God's "living waters."

* * *

Whoever drinks of the water that I shall give him will never thirst; the water that I shall give him will become in him a spring of water welling up to eternal life (John 4:14).

SCRIPTURE READING: John 4:7-26

PRAYER: Gracious and omniscient God, our Father, who hast placed strong desires within us so that we might seek after thee and live, let us not be satisfied with anything that weakens our bodies, that poisons our minds, or that stunts our souls. May we taste and see how good thou art in the life of Jesus Christ our Lord. Amen.

A BORROWED LIGHT

Swiftly an ominous storm thundered upon us late in the afternoon, twelve miles from home. Within minutes we were in boat and canoe moving rapidly among bending reeds and leaping waves of an ordinarily placid river which connects two favorite lakes. For the sake of guests and their children, we stopped at a cabin at the mouth of the river. No one was at home, but we found shelter in a large boat-house, as wet darkness lowered upon us.

Unfortunately we had forgotten our flashlights when we left our cabin in the bright morning hours. When the storm had passed, the rain persisted and we cut across the lake to the nearest camp to borrow a light for the long journey home. Flashes of lightning prevented some of our encounters with rocks and reefs from becoming disastrous. When we were able to procure a light, our way home in the night rain was made safer. No longer did our boat and canoe drift apart, and the buoys and rocks were recognized. When at midnight the outline of our pier and cabin could be discerned, we were especially thankful for the borrowed light.

Every cry of pain or distress, every shout of cynicism or ignorance, every call in darkness or confusion, is at heart someone saying: "Lend me a light." Fortunate are we when there is someone to encourage and befriend us, someone whose life is like a shining encampment of faith from which we may borrow a light until we hold our own steadily and securely.

Sometimes our planning for living proves inadequate. Events come upon us unexpectedly. We are put to the test among strange experiences, unfamiliar places, and unknown people. How relieved we are when someone can counsel us in such a predicament with insights from the Eternal, and we say: "Thy word is a lamp to my feet and a light to my path" (Psalm 119:105).

There are moments when it is wise to wait until the tempest subsides and we regain our bearings. It is difficult to think when anger is aroused, when emotions are at high pitch or when the shock of disappointment leaves us stunned. The patience and self-control of a friend may become a borrowed ray which restores perspective.

Perhaps we do not have enough light to see a way beyond disagreements or differing points of view which threaten to separate us. Yet someone with forbearance bravely extends a hand in the spirit of reconciliation, and it becomes indeed a borrowed light.

Or we may be exposed to the winds of an evil influence and to the drift of the crowd. We are wavering in indecision. One person speaks with conviction. He is like a light—and more—he gives us something inspiring to take along.

One of the many tributes given Jesus was that "the common people heard him gladly" (Mark 12:37). Strange situations and unconventional circumstances presented themselves as opportunities in which he could reveal a light from God. He was not merely interested in exposing what people lacked. His was a passion to add brightness of life to every soul. No wonder that after beholding his restoring love, his boundless kindness, and his mastery of life, the disciple John remembers him as "the Light of the World." Christ had few things which he could call his own. But one thing he could always share with others—that was the Light of Life.

The most convincing inducement to faith in God is not a clever philosophical argument but another faith which thinks, loves, and ventures in his name. Is not our own faith one which God lighted with someone else's life? It is a shared faith which binds us together. "For he who does not love his brother whom he has seen, cannot love God whom he has not seen" (1 John 4:20). A light can make the difference between crashing on reefs in the darkness and coming home safely. What a privilege to lend a light!

*   *   *

We love, because he first loved us (1 John 4:19).

SCRIPTURE READING: 1 John 4:7-21

PRAYER: Forbid, O Lord, that if anyone wavers, we should not stand firm; if anyone waits for strength, we should withdraw our hand; if anyone is discouraged, we should not speak words which uphold; if anyone is lost, we should not share a light and if anyone seeks thee, we should fail to let our faith shine. We praise thee that in Christ thy Light of Life is shining and that the darkness cannot put it out. Amen.

STORM-FELLED

Ominous, black clouds rolled in from the southeast. Most storms originate from angles of the north, west, and south. This storm coming from an easterly direction made up for rare incidence with accumulated vengeance. We were thankful when it was spent and our cabin was spared.

The following day our canoe skimmed over water reflecting shoreline images and storm-strewn flotsam. We were taking inventory of the storm's damage on familiar island scenes. The number of green trees blown down made us wonder why they fell while others remained standing.

One large tree was felled although its roots reached deep into the ground. Curiously, however, its roots had grown toward only two opposing directions while the other two sides remained devoid of roots. The storm from the southeast had surprised this tree by blowing where it had no strength to hold and no power to brace. The tree was unprepared for winds approaching from unusual directions.

Have we not similarly been caught off guard by some storms of temptation because their nature and direction were not foreseen? Temptations do not always strike on the side where we are best fortified in conviction and experience. Evil likes to attack or seduce on the weak side of human nature. Our faith cannot afford to be one-sided in its guarding of life. We need to grow roots into all areas of living, reinforced for good and evil weather.

Some trees obviously fell because they had grown on a rocky shelf on which roots formed a large, shallow mat. The pressure of the wind was greater than the holding power of all the roots and, as a result, some pines thirty or forty years of age fell prematurely. A superficial preparation for life may not be exposed for years. Shallow thoughts, a lack of knowledge about the Christian life, ignorance about the truths of the Bible, a refusal to let faith lead into intimate relationship with God, are all weaknesses exposed in the testing of stormy days. Even God would not keep a life with shallow roots standing.

There were some trees that had stood next to an area where lumber had been harvested. Not mature enough for cutting, these trees had been spared the lumberman's ax but now had fallen. They had depended upon older and larger trees to protect them from strong winds. Now they were not ready to stand alone. Where life is expected to favor and coddle us, there the blessings of strength are missed.

Character, like strength, must be developed. We are not automatically prepared for life upon reaching the age of twenty-one nor upon graduating from college. Rather, we must learn to stand on our own feet, and we must do our own thinking and believing if we are to grow and stand in the strength and stature of the Christian life.

*   *   *

That you, being rooted and grounded in love, may have power to comprehend with all the saints what is the breadth and length and height and depth, and to know the love of Christ which surpasses knowledge (Eph. 3:17b-19a).

SCRIPTURE READING: Ephesians 6:10-17

PRAYER: Strong Son of God, save us from overestimating our strength and teach us to look to thy example of faith in facing evil, facing the cross, and facing death. Grant us power to hold fast to the things which endure; we ask it in thy name. Amen.

DESIGN FOR SURVIVAL

The sudden whirr of wings and the detracting call of a grouse hen, while her chicks scurry for cover of leaves and camouflage of underbrush, is a fascinating study in patterns for survival. It is one of many methods through which animals and birds manage to preserve their existence. Some of them blend into the surroundings through brilliant or drab colorations; others, like ducks, are counter-shaded, as disruptive colorations make tracing difficult among rays of light on dark forest ground. Different are porcupine with needles and the skunk with scent, making proximity unpleasant for dangerous visitors. A turtle can crawl into its portable house, a chipmunk scampers into a hole and a squirrel finds security in a tall tree. While deer or fox may

run away swiftly, an opossum plays dead. Instinctively each species of life reacts with its own pattern for survival.

Man also has many threats to life and security. However, he has to reckon with the survival of both the body and the spirit. History is, in part, the record of the struggle between the survival of the strong and the weak, the good and the evil. The technique for self-preservation has ranged from war and refuge to absorption and compromise. Our methods are not instinctive but similar to or a combination of those of the animals. Yet ours is the obligation of choosing to what degree our pattern of survival shall rise above the animal and reveal a design consistent with the life of the spirit.

There are times when the survival patterns for the continuation of physical life and comfort conflict with the preservation of conscience and faith. The clamor for outward well-being is loudest. Because it is visible, the physical structure of the body, family, church, community, and nation makes its insistent appeal. We are, therefore, confronted with questions: "Are superiority in destructive rocket power and adequacy of bomb shelters enough for survival? Or are the faith in democracy, the vitality of church membership, the sincere quest for truth, and the outgoing concern for fellowman the final determiners for survival? What do we want to have survive? With what would we like to establish ourselves?"

A watchful deer, standing among trees on the water's edge as the sun goes down, is not easy to spot. Wild ducks, camouflaged among rocks of the shoreline, are not spied

readily. It is tragic when it is hard to spot a Christian because he blends in perfectly with what everybody else is
doing and thinking. Oddly enough, a Christian is in danger
of extinction if he is not willing when required to stand
against a temptation, to vote alone, to speak out, and to be
recognized. Nicodemus "came to Jesus by night." The saints,
on the other hand, have always been clumsy at camouflag-
ing their faith or in disguising their way. The layman
Stephen, stoned to death for his unrelenting faith in Christ,
became the first Christian martyr and was identified until
his last breath as loving his enemies. A man named Saul
found that this was a sure way by which faith survives.

The art of running from danger has also been adopted by
many human beings. All of us find that we are experts in the
art of evading responsibility for a good cause. Time,
strength, and love are withheld or withdrawn. How often a
worthy enterprise or noble endeavor suffers because of the
evasiveness of those who are gifted with intelligence, resources, and talents but are not dedicated. They shy from
getting involved in the problems of human need and faith
and consequently have no part in the Christian design for
survival. Sad is the report: "Then all the disciples forsook
him and fled" (Matt. 26:56b). But a later testimony identifies their faith distinctly: "Now when they saw the boldness
of Peter and John . . . they recognized that they had been
with Jesus" (Acts 4:13).

A lynx lives by its leap to kill. A Christian lives by his
willingness to let something die within himself so that there
may be life for others and himself. "Only let your manner

of life be worthy of the gospel of Christ, . . . not frightened in anything by your opponents." These are the farewell words of the man who once persecuted Stephen. On another occasion he says: "'If your enemy is hungry, feed him; if he is thirsty, give him drink'; . . . Do not be overcome by evil, but overcome evil with good" (Rom. 12:20-21). History has shown that not opposition but prosperity and conformity have often weakened the faith and courage of the Christian fellowship. A self-giving spirit and a devotion in the name of the cross are still the Christian's design for survival. "If any man would come after me, let him deny himself and take up his cross and follow me" (Matt. 16:24).

* * *

Only let your manner of life be worthy of the gospel of Christ, . . . not frightened in anything by your opponents (Phil. 1:27-28a).

SCRIPTURE READING: 1 Corinthians 1:22-31

PRAYER: Dear Father, fill us with thy Spirit that inwardly and outwardly we may be one in purpose to do thy will, to be faithful in our love and to show, in living or in dying, that thy life is gain in this world and in the world to come; through Jesus Christ our Lord. Amen.

THUNDER AND LIGHTNING

There is a majestic and other-worldly grandeur about a thunder storm in midsummer. All the vast powers of the heavens and the earth present themselves in dramatic conflict. When the woods are tinder-dry and the underbrush wilts in noonday heat we have the scenic background for the prologue of waiting for the storm.

The setting for the first act is a hot and humid atmosphere, in which life is restless and uncomfortable. The birds fly low and uneasiness grips man and beast. Little tree toads triple-tongue their notes to release tension as ominous clouds begin to raise the horizon in the storm corner. The second act opens as turbulent clouds of black-gray and blue-green cast appear to race like horses and chariots under the command of the voice of thunder. Sea gulls sweep upward in excitement upon the wind currents. Birch and aspen bend over as if the forest were fleeing from the oncoming storm.

The climax comes in the third act when the lightning swiftly thrusts its swords of fire across the distant heavens. The wind now whips a watrous apron of torrential rain, and the lightning strikes near with fearful and shattering effect. Large hail falls, and the surface of the lake begins to leap and spurt upward. Suddenly a blazing lightning bolt strikes a favorite tall pine and splinters it from top to bottom, demonstrating a power beyond our prediction and control.

The epilogue, a vivid contrast to the awesome terror and violence, appears in the brightness and calm that follow. Hearts are filled with thanksgiving to God who has again watered and refreshed the earth. No one would think of separating the storm and fallen trees from any of the acts or the epilogue.

Nature responds to physical laws without partiality, and the rain and sunshine fall on the just and the unjust. Primitive man looked in vain to nature for a reassuring word from God about love, suffering, righteousness, life, and death. In superstition and dread he associated storm, sunshine, and animals with good and evil spirits. But such spirits were of his own imagining and could not respond to his moral or spiritual needs.

The Bible is unique as inspired literature because in and through it God speaks to every human spiritual struggle in the midst of sunshine and of storm. The fellowship of the church relives and retells this drama of life and faith for each generation.

Thunder was heard when Moses received the Ten Commandments. When men like Samuel, Elijah, and Amos spoke, thunder and lightning were signs of God's support of righteousness and of his judgment upon evil. No one could escape the eye or the will of the Eternal.

Today many people find the biblical faith difficult to accept because they desire only a "sunshine faith." They want no "thunder and lightning" experience which acknowledges God's judgment upon their lives. They are ready to receive divine love, kindness, and blessings, and are quick to call for God's judgment upon the obvious sins of other people. That the love and judgment of God always belong together as surely as sunshine and lightning is difficult for them to understand. Nevertheless, divine love is not sentimental or weak. Life is not just a beautiful "epilogue" but a facing of all of God's seasons and weather for living.

The great darkness over the earth with its violent upheavals at the time of Jesus' crucifixion is a physical picture of how the judgment of the Man upon the cross has reverberated upon the conscience and soul of mankind. We see righteous love showing up evil for what it really is and what it does to the goodness of God in Christ. Jesus exposes the hatefulness and doom of sin before all creation.

The Christ upon the tree revealed something infinitely more momentous than the fact that the thunder and lightning of God's judgment had struck mankind upon a hill called Golgotha. As we feel a terrifying nearness in our own soul to the sins which crucified our Lord, we cry out, "If thou, O Lord, shouldst mark iniquities, Lord, who could stand?" (Ps. 130:3). It is at this point that a wonderful and unparalleled revelation of God breaks through with the saving word of the Gospel. The love which lets its lightning of judgment fall upon sinners is also the love which identifies itself with us and arrests the destroying "lightning" to transform it into the light of God's forgiving mercy. The love of God rejects and convicts evil and at the same time actively reaches out to reconcile and to redeem. "Behold the goodness and severity of God" in the grace of our Lord Jesus Christ.

*   *   *

For God sent the Son into the world, not to condemn the world, but that the world might be saved through him (John 3:17).

SCRIPTURE READING: Job 28:25-28; Romans 11:33-36

PRAYER: Merciful God, our Father, whose love is great beyond our understanding, we adore thee for the gift of mercy and life in thy Son for all thy children. In his suffering, our denials and betrayals of thee are shamed. Forgive our sins and help us to follow thee with a love which knows our weakness and thy strength; through Jesus Christ our Lord. Amen.

THE UNLOCKED DOOR

Occasionally a hunter or traveler loses his way in the wilderness. Hunger, cold, and animals become a serious threat to health and safety unless adequate food and shelter can be procured.

In an isolated northern area an owner of a cabin was thoughtfully concerned about this danger to lost wanderers. When he closed up after the summer season, he left the outside door to the kitchen unlocked and fastened only the inner door leading to the other portion of the cabin. He stored dried foods, a few blankets as well as firewood in the kitchen. His cabin became a potential rescue post to unknown travelers.

The example of the "unlocked door" illustrates a fundamental attitude in Christian giving and service. This kind of uncalculating generosity and simple trust, demonstrated in providing friendly shelter, is at the heart of all Christian charity. It possessed the power of imagination to look beyond one's own needs and enjoyment to the plight of a fellowman. Here was no request for publicity or for compensation. This gracious spirit was not limited to friends during a vacation but continued to meet even the unseen stranger.

The cabin owner risked much by leaving his door unlocked and in offering hospitality and aid. Vandals might have taken advantage of his kindness and could have destroyed the property. People may have accepted the hospitality without deserving it. But the risk was worth taking for the sake of the one lost traveler who might be helped.

The element of risk is always found in every kind of charitable endeavor. Everyone who loves may "get hurt"; everyone who extends a hand may receive a bruise. The danger of being misunderstood or unappreciated is ever present. Some of the finest humanitarian projects and noblest missionary ventures were judged failures by popular standards. What we contribute may not bring about the results we anticipate. Some disappointed or embittered people consequently refuse to love and to give.

Such fear and reluctance forgets that the spirit of adventure is needed as much in Christian benevolence and service as in fighting the enemies of faith. Doors to new fields of service and for new ways of helping fellowmen in the areas of human wilderness wait to be opened. We must examine frequently the method and goal of missionary, social, educational, and charitable work in church and community. Unreserved love and generosity will not be discouraged or disqualified by some failures.

To help someone costs something. Think of noble men and women who blessed mankind and one has a catalogue of hardships. They spent something of self, incurred discomforts, or sacrificed life to unlock a door for some new benefit, some saving word or some light for those in distress.

The Good Shepherd did not spare himself so that his sheep might enter the door of the sheepfold. To believe in a Christ who gave his life for us and then to claim that life in his name costs nothing is pitifully inconsistent. The Good Samaritan kept the door of the inn open for further help to the victim when he instructed the innkeeper, "Take care of him; and whatever more you spend, I will repay you when I come back" (Luke 10:35b).

A great deterrent to a generous and uncalculating attitude is ridicule. We do not like to be regarded "foolish" or "unreasonable." A particularly vicious sort of ridicule against those engaging in brotherly ventures among different races, in new fields, or in distant nations is the label "do-gooders." Labels are attached incorrectly by the unthinking and the unloving. Our Lord, according to Luke, "went about doing good" (Acts 10:38).

The selfish and irreverent insist upon quick results and immediate rewards. Jesus' parable of the tares (Matt. 13:24-43) teaches us that for the present time the good and the evil will go in and out of the same door until the day of reckoning. Jesus opened doors of God's love and mercy, not because he knew so little but because he knew so much.

*　　*　　*

I was a stranger and you welcomed me (Matt. 25:35).

SCRIPTURE READING: Matthew 25:31-46

PRAYER: God our Father, who withholdest no good thing from thy children and desirest that our hearts be open to one another's need, bestow such love upon us that we may serve thee with abandon and do good with joy; through Jesus Christ our Lord. Amen.

A DOUBLE RAINBOW

A rainbow is so ephemeral in beauty and infrequent in appearance that even those who have seen its heavenly arched colors for many summers look up with the young in admiration. How delicate are its pure hues of light shining through tiny watrous lenses of rain and mist!

One summer day after a heavy rainstorm we saw the rare phenomenon of an almost perfect double rainbow. The lower, clearer arch, with its red color on the outer edge and violet color within, touched the horizons from end to end. The faint, higher bow, with the colors inverted, was distinct in its sweep until it neared the earth. We were enthralled.

What must primitive people throughout the world have thought of this arch of fleeting glory? It appeared frequently after storms and catastrophes with their aftermath of destruction, flood, and death. The early Hebrew people interpreted the events of nature, as well as the events of history, in the perspective of faith in the one God who rules over all things.

The grandeur of the rainbow is associated with an early Bible story. "The Lord saw that the wickedness of man was great in the earth and that every imagination of the thoughts of his heart was only evil continually" (Gen. 6:5). In this account, only Noah and his family were spared in a great flood in which all the people perished. This remarkable story of hope ends with the telling of a most significant event. God makes a covenant with Noah and his descendants. It bespoke an entirely different relationship between God and his people than between the pagan gods and their worshippers. The latter lived in continual dread and uncertainty. They expected their deities to be capricious and vindictive. But those who from the days of Noah and Abraham had followed the living God in faith, found a new kind of trust-relationship. In the history of Judaism and Christianity it has been characteristic that vital religion was a personal bond between God and people.

The great prophets declared that as surely as the rainbow appeared to every generation of men, so God renewed the broken covenant with his children. The freeing of Israel from slavery in Egypt and her establishment in the Promised Land was a symbol of God's supreme favor. He had blessed them abundantly and kept his promises to them. Consequently, he expected more from them in moral and spiritual response than from any other people in the world.

What was once symbolized by the rainbow became a part of the ceremonies, observances, and sacred writings of the people. The prophet Hosea, for example, let his own tragic experience dramatize anew the significant depth and intimacy of the covenant bond with God. His own wife had been faithless, and he bought her back out of slavery and brought her home. From this recurring sorrow he gained a profound spiritual insight into God's relationship with his people. In moving words he hears God say: "And I will betroth you to me for ever; I will betroth you to me in righteousness and in justice, in steadfast love and in mercy. I will betroth you to me in faithfulness; and you shall know the Lord" (Hosea 2:19-20). The rainbow, with its associations of God's mercy and faithfulness in the Old Covenant, is followed by the revelations of the Gospel story of the New Covenant. The life and redemption in Christ confront us with even more intimate obligations and sacred relationships entrusted by the Eternal.

Brilliant and powerful as the sun's light may be, a rainbow lasts only as long as raindrops filter the magnificent miracle of light. This intimate and immediate relationship with God is symbolized and reenacted in the celebration of the Lord's Supper. Here the New Covenant is personalized through the awareness of the presence of Christ who has dominion over evil and who has revealed his covenanting bond through his life, death, and resurrection. The rainbow reaches from refreshed fields to the bread and cup with which we celebrate God's triumphant new life in Christ and our receiving of it in faithfulness.

*   *   *

Be faithful unto death, and I will give you the crown of life. (Rev. 2:10).

SCRIPTURE READING: 1 Corinthians 11:23-28

PRAYER: O God our Father, who hast given us abundant gifts in thy creation and immeasurable gifts of life through thy grace in Jesus Christ, grant us fullness of the power of thy Spirit so that having received much we may be found faithful and loving in all things; through Jesus Christ our Lord. Amen.

PINE CONES

Some pines tower above others in the forest, giving the impression that they have always been standing there. Among the top branches are hundreds of green cones, some in clusters, which seem more ornate than useful. After two years of growth, the ripened cones open and small seeds come swirling to the soft duff. Contrary to first impressions, these cones with their precious hoard are the promise and beginning of trees and of forests for generations to come.

The simple lesson of the pines and their seed-laden cones is not so evident in matters of the Christian life and faith to our swift-moving, transplanted generation. Today most families do not have a strong sense of interdependence in the stages of planting, cultivating, and seed-bearing of Christian nurture. A perspective which embraces several generations of the family, and the consequences of their faithful or faithless living, is continually disrupted. We see only cones, or only saplings, or only a giant tree without relating the life of one to the other.

It is alarming that a generation which is engrossed with scientific knowledge about every phase of the propagation of the human race, dedicates comparatively little energy, time, and resources to the furthering of Christian thought and its heritage. We live in a land where worship of God and expression of faith are unrestricted by law. But our religious freedom dare not be identified with a careless handling of the gifts of the Spirit for young and old. The perpetuation of the Christian interpretation of life cannot be taken for granted. Even as millions of seeds of the conifers are eaten by birds and rodents, so there are competitive interests and false standards which daily devour seeds blown by the winds of the Spirit of God toward children and adults. Valued seeds of faith and tender growth in love toward God and man need protection and cultivation.

Young souls may be blighted by the family which lives as if there were no God. Of course, no teacher or parent can "produce" faith or "make" a Christian. Yet prayerful influence is conducive to the beautiful unfolding of life. The potentials of a character may be given opportunity to take root. Seedlings may be moved out of smothering shade into God's light. Thus God needed Joseph and Mary, who took the child Jesus and fled from the vicious Herod to Egypt where the child could "increase."

The jack pine cones are different from those of the white and Norway pines, the balsam and spruce. Small in size, they are hard as knots and are difficult to open. Heat of forest fires, hot sunshine, or saturating ground moisture eventually cause the release of the seed. In life also there are hidden potentials which usual experience and training do not evoke. A crisis, a struggle, a loss, or a challenge is needed before the seeds find "good ground" in which to sprout. Though the process may be later and slower in life, the occasion does not produce the seed but opens it. Without cones even the jack pines would die out. Without knowledge and experience of the Christian faith the most opportune circumstances for living may prove barren.

Jesus did not mature as an isolated youth even though he had a singular mission. He shared the inspiring family worship; he built articles with integrity in the carpenter shop; he received the counsel of the Law and the word of the prophets. It was not by chance that "the child grew and became strong, filled with wisdom; and the favor of God was upon him" (Luke 2:40). Precious pine cones borne high on boughs of tall trees make us mindful how a Christian life and a community of faith come into being and continue to live.

*   *   *

And those who are wise shall shine like the brightness of the firmament; and those who turn many to righteousness, like the stars for ever and ever (Dan. 12:3).

SCRIPTURE READING: 1 Timothy 4:7-12

PRAYER: God our Father, we stand in awe before each mind and soul, for they are thy handiwork. We do not know what wondrous thoughts and influence thy Spirit would inspire. Keep us from causing anyone to stumble. Help us to learn and to teach in the spirit of Jesus Christ our Lord. Amen.

PARASITES

For centuries the Niagara Falls barred the sea lamprey, native to the Atlantic Ocean, from inhabiting the upper lakes. When the Welland Canal was dug for ships, it also provided a migratory stream for the sea lamprey to come all the way through Lake Erie and Lake Huron to Lake Superior, with its shore-line of wilderness. The lamprey, being a parasite, attached itself to the lake trout, sucking out strength and life. The scourge multiplied phenomenally, thereby increasing its detrimental threat and effect. Fishermen were deprived of their trade, sportsmen found the trout season closed, and a delectable fish was no longer generally available.

The word parasite, of Greek derivation, describes a repulsive trait found also among humans. It signified one who flattered and amused his host in return for free meals. A parasite lives on someone or something else without giving anything sustaining in return. Plants bearing beautiful flowers may attach themselves to trees, roots, or stalks and steal life-giving energy. Mosses may kill the tree they adorn. In

113

human relationships those who prey upon lives and values are as varied as parasites in nature.

Communities as well as nations are vulnerable to miserable robbers of the strength of civic decency, of fellow-feeling, and of discerning conscience. Wrecked, weakened, and dissipated human beings are left in the wake of narcotics, gambling, prostitution, alcoholism, racketeering, and many other vicious perversions.

How would you like to belong to a fellowship of parasites? One shudders at the thought of living with people, each suspicious of the other and with no sense of family or of belonging together. They would be a collection of individuals without a sense of gratitude for nurture, care, and love. Such a lecherous group would devitalize all that sustains and nourishes mind and soul.

We would be unrealistic if we glibly dismissed the threat of this evil just because it has not appeared in its worst forms among us. The sea lamprey which reached Lake Superior swam through an innocent-looking canal. An old Jewish proverb recognized how such a grasping spirit drains life out of everyday relationships: "The leech has two daughters; 'Give, give,' they cry" (Prov. 30:15a). The social climber and the covetous seeker of privilege, who are unwilling to earn esteem and trust, chant those words. The demands of wife or husband, the "gim-me gim-me" of teenagers, the whining of children increase the volume. Those who evade responsibilities of work and of study, of decisions and of trust, are like the cowbird which expects other birds to hatch the eggs she has laid in their nests. "Let the church teach faith to my child." "Let the government provide." "We have that coming." So life is supposed to owe all a living but all of us are immeasurably in debt to life.

Are we not less than human when the unattractive spirit of parasites grips us? "Happiness was born twins," because we were created to receive and to give in the sight of God and fellowman. Ours is only half a life when limited to selfish receiving. God is no fool to be pleased by flattery. In his mercy he is always ready to fill our empty lives with joy and with good things when we come to him humbly and in faith.

Those who have a self-effacing devotion to a cause set our hearts afire. Those who have a passion for the good have a convincing verdict for living. Christ humbled himself to share with us the help and gifts of God. His Spirit still says, "Come over to help us" across lake or ocean.

*   *   *

Do nothing from selfishness or conceit, but in humility count others better than yourselves (Phil. 2:3).

SCRIPTURE READING: Philippians 2:4-11

PRAYER: O God, the Father of us all, without whose love no gift gains true worth, we are weary and ashamed of our selfish life. Grant us humility of heart so that thy Spirit may take the place of laziness, of dullness, and of pride. Forgive our self-centeredness or we die. Help us to find that life which is inwardly rich, which lives as it shares, and which finds joy in the Lord of life; in Jesus' name. Amen.

A TRIP INTO THE WILDERNESS

There are matchless wilderness scenes of rare beauty in the Quetico-Superior country which are inaccessible except by canoe and portage. Streams cascading over rapids, furtive wild life in the thick forest edge, chains of lakes with infinite variations of shorelines and cliffs, all present an exhilarating invitation to an adventure of inward and outward renewal.

Planning for a canoe trip is a parable for living. Only the foolish would venture upon a long trek into the wild forest without careful preparation. It could prove costly and dangerous if excitement and anticipation took the place of plans and preparation. To peruse a canoe map and find bewitching names of lakes such as Ogishkemuncie, Saganaga, and Gabemichigama dare not obscure the fact that hazards which may disrupt a journey often lurk disarmingly amidst the things we most enjoy. The adventure of finding new meaning for one's vocation requires more than emotional response. Exploring the implications of the spirit of love and justice demands more than enthusiastic assent. Faith claims not only the heart but the head. The best cause needs prayerful thought which looks to the farthest end of the journey.

116

Not until the first portage of a mile or more does one appreciate compactness and lightness in a packsack. The uninitiated are tempted to take along too much. We are not always wise enough to recognize this fact in the Christian life. John Bunyan, in his allegory *Pilgrim's Progress* emphasizes that those who wanted to take along every luxury and enjoyment on their journey to the heavenly city dropped out by the wayside.

We must determine, then, whether a pleasure, a comfort, or an interest is a deterrent or even an unmanageable burden as we pursue our portage of hope and faith. "Let us also lay aside every weight, and sin which clings so closely, and let us run with perseverance the race that is set before us, looking to Jesus the pioneer and perfecter of our faith" (Heb. 12:1b-2a). Self-indulgence has canceled many an expedition into the good life. More people have exhausted themselves by shouldering "unnecessary weight" in living than in carrying what our Lord requires of us.

There are essentials for a canoe trip: dry foods and concentrates; light utensils and fishing equipment; a tent with sleeping bag and useful clothing; and also a first-aid kit, knife, hatchet, matches, flashlight, and map. Have you ever made a list of what you regard as indispensable among the possessions and activities which absorb your physical, mental, and inner energies? What demands your time? It is amazing how many of the essential things in the Christian life are "light." Faith in God is light, weighed against worldly goods; concern for others is no load in contrast to dominating ambition; forgiveness lightens the heart over against

a heavy grudge; a prayer is light, compared to proud self-sufficiency. The fundamentals of our faith carry well and are imperishable. But it requires time and careful selection before we acquire the inner grace to see the things "God has prepared for those who love him" (1 Cor. 2:9).

It is both amusing and pitiable to meet someone on a portage cursing the wilderness because he is miserable with his pack. In the midst of glorious beauty and wondrous things he feels cheated. He wants a soda in the wilderness when he can drink refreshing waters. An unhappy, complaining Christian is just as pitiable and ridiculous. He complains because there are not shortcuts or exemptions in burden-bearing. His eyes are upon a blister rather than upon the joy and purpose of life in the kingdom. The Apostle Paul, in the midst of difficult journeys on rugged land and on high seas, gives us a clue to inner preparation: "I know how to be abased, and I know how to abound; in any and all circumstances I have learned the secret of facing plenty and hunger, abundance and want. I can do all things in him who strengthens me" (Phil. 4:12-13).

*　　*　　*

But as for you, man of God, shun all this; aim at righteousness, godliness, faith, love, steadfastness, gentleness (1 Tim. 6:11).

SCRIPTURE READING: 1 Timothy 6:9-12

PRAYER: God our Father, we pray that the cares of this world may not hide thy care for us and that the riches of the earth may never distract us from the treasures within thy kingdom. Grant us discernment to reject what hinders and to select those gifts which will help us to walk with joy until our pilgrimage is ended and we come safely unto thee; through Jesus Christ our Lord. Amen.

LIKE AN EAGLE

The small river widened into an area of muskeg and water-grass. Red-winged blackbirds and meadowlarks, perched on scraggy spruce and tamarack, gladdened us by their flutter and song. In the distance stood a crane, apparently asleep while on sentinel duty. Then he heard our paddle strokes and lifted cumbersome wings in low flight. Around the next bend of the river a secluded lake beckoned us. We lifted our eyes and observed an eagle in the blue heavens. How gracefully he soared! What mastery and strength in effortless flight!

We hoped to remain unobserved, but a scream in high air warned us that sharp eyes had caught our movement. The eagle flew directly to a tall dead tree on the right, and we paddled in close to the shore. Thus hidden, we skimmed quietly past a dense wall of trees until by general estimate we were in line with the tall perch. Then we turned slowly at a right angle into the lake and peered carefully over the tree tops until we spied the regal, defiant bird. Simultaneously each of us stifled surprise—farther back was the nest of the eagle in another towering pine.

Eagles are renowned for superb strength and skill in flight. They dive fiercely upon prey and have power to lift heavy bounty as they fly high and far. They are also known for rare tenderness to their brood. When the eaglets have attained a certain age, a parent bird stirs up the nest. The offspring must learn at great risk to spread their wings. Flight which later follows so naturally and smoothly is at first forced upon them. If they were never pushed out of their secure environment, they might not learn to use their tremendous wings.

The mother eagle knows that her young were made to fly as no other bird. Combined with what seems to be a ruthless gesture is the remarkable maneuver of the parent bird as it flies protectively beside its fluttering young, ready to sweep beneath and carry with strong wings.

The Bible likens some of the attributes of God to a living stream, a majestic mountain, or a mighty rock. It also refers to God as a dove, describing the quiet, peaceful, and gracious influence of his Spirit. In contrast, God is also "like an eagle that stirs up its nest, that flutters over its young, spreading out its wings, catching them, bearing them on its pinions" (Deut. 32:11-12b).

These exquisite lines recall that God watched over Israel as an eagle watches over its young. He did not permit his people to remain in the security of Egypt, but pushed them out of their "nest" where they had not learned to use their wings of freedom. Many were afraid to "fly" through the long wilderness to a new destiny in the Promised Land. They preferred the safety of the "flesh-pots" and forgot that their bodies and souls were enslaved. God's doing seemed cruel to them even as it does to us when we are "pushed out" of a comfortable nest of habit, mediocrity, and tradition. We like to cling to security even when our spirits were made to fly high and far into the unknown. Someone wiser than we "stirs up the nest." God wants us to develop as his children and "it does not yet appear what we shall be" (1 John 3:2).

If we want to discover our vocation in life and develop our talents, we must trust God as we try our wings. The experience will be strange and frightening. We may wonder and doubt when nothing seems to support us. Yet God is like an eagle bearing us "on his wings."

There are two ways of interpreting history. One says, "We have been pushed out of our nest . . . life is ruthless and without undergirding." The other holds the faith that God's Spirit prods us to live beyond an earthbound nest and to reach for the qualities which belong to the kingdom of heaven.

The eagle resumed his flight, soared many minutes without movement of wings, and then rose deftly against a strong wind current. It reminded us of the Master, who like a lone eagle of the Spirit, flew against the forces of evil and revealed the soaring might of God's redemptive love. Man, too, was intended to soar by faith in God's power to overcome evil. The human spirit can rise to heights against opposition when it trusts God to carry.

*   *   *

They who wait for the Lord shall renew their strength, they shall mount up with wings like eagles, they shall run and not be weary, they shall walk and not faint (Isa. 40:31).

SCRIPTURE READING: Psalm 91

PRAYER: Everlasting God, our Father, thou who dost support the worlds in their flight, grant us grace to entrust our lives to thine everlasting arms. Forgive our faint-heartedness. Help us to rise in the full stature of faith and to reach out into new and unknown areas of life where thou desirest us to learn, love, and serve; through Jesus Christ our Lord. Amen.

SUNRISE AND SUNSET

The wonder and splendor of the rising and setting of the sun were meant for the eye and the spirit of every man. The sky does not ring bells to call our hearts to nature's matins or vespers. It relies on the silent rhapsody of color to create the mood of adoration. Many are the beautiful scenes in high mountains or quiet valleys which inspire the spirit of awe. But the glorious riot of color in the morning and the fading evening grandeur offer the finest moments for adoration. Not all eyes are imbued with the spirit of reverence as they behold this miracle of beauty which caresses earth and water and sky. Some see only the sun and clouds over forest or lake, but sunrise and sunset are given to us by God our Father that we may learn to adore him in his mystery and majesty.

Our spirit is overwhelmed by the day's prelude and post-lude of light, magnificent beyond anything that man can create or conceive. What we are and what we have done— even what we hope to do—dwindles into insignificance. "This is the Lord's doing; it is marvelous in our eyes" (Psalm 118:23). Intuitively we sense that this is happening to us because God is alive. Can anything be compared to his infinite wisdom and power? We are not at the center of this pageant, and we have prepared nothing for it. This is God's rapture in mother-of-pearl and golden light, in roseate hues, and purple blends of glory.

As we stand before these footlights to God's throne, a chastened attitude brings a reversal of our view toward life and of our part in it. Our preoccupation with self embar-rasses us. We are invited to adore the wondrous and holy God.

Adoration is such a simple, spontaneous, and quiet re-sponse to God that its importance easily escapes us. Through it our attention is captured by God, and we forget anxieties and frustrations. Moments of awe are not the time to ponder problems. We wait for that which the splendor of a Presence would impart. We cease trying to influence God and we stop bartering for favors. Our awareness of being is immersed in wonder. What we think and want is no longer important in this moment. The tense grip is released; we fold our hands, and our soul whispers: "Holy, holy, holy, Lord God of hosts, heaven and earth are full of thy glory" (Isa. 6:3).

The spirit of adoration is often ignored as a significant element of prayer; it imparts the proper focus to praise, petition, intercession, and dedication. In adoration a sense of awe possesses us, hallowing all other portions of the heart's conversation with God. The center of prayer is no longer "I" but "Thou." Our lips refuse to whisper, "God, I want this" but rather, "I am thine, use me Lord."

What we behold in nature's splendor is like a stairway to the altar of God. As we kneel there, we find a life and a cross which invite us to behold the light shining from God's kingdom. To stand before the moral beauty of Christ's life and to behold the wonder of his love and goodness is to adore the very nature of God. His is the radiance of the Eternal upon the earth; it is redeeming splendor in human form; it is the glorious life of the Spirit shining among us. Sunrise and sunset remind us that the beginning and the end of everything in our life is to be suffused daily by the marvelous, restoring life of God. He who adores becomes humble and receptive, as well as obedient and joyous.

❋   ❋   ❋

Holy, holy, holy is the Lord God Almighty, who was and is and is to come (Rev. 4:8b).

SCRIPTURE READING: Psalm 113:1-6

PRAYER: Hush our hearts, O God, and possess our souls until we are lost in wonder, love and praise; through Jesus Christ our Lord. Amen.

THE STARS IN THEIR COURSES

Friends were sitting with us on the rock terrace near the cabin in the cool evening breeze. In silence we watched the shadows play their beauty upon the straits and forest. As crickets and frogs began their evening incantations, our guests told their story. They recalled how a large, useful community building at a mission station had been destroyed by an angry mob. Simple, trusting people were incited by grandiose and false promises. Slow and hard-won attainments were ridiculed. Evil motives were imputed to Christian leaders, and within a few swift, terrible minutes the work of a lifetime lay in ashes.

A sad, pensive mood possessed us as we contemplated the sinister event. It was dark now, and the stars that had appeared one by one were surrounded by a shimmering multitude. A rebel meteor flashed across the night sky. Its brief, blazing path did not disturb the North Star, the Big Dipper, Cassiopeia, and their companions. Northern lights began to flash up and down on low heavens in greenish-yellow hues. We thought of the fires of destruction in the faraway country and then looked at the stars again.

It is said that in the day the sun casts light for everyone in general; but the stars appear to shine upon us individually. This evening they had a personal, coded signal out of eternity.

We remembered lines from Deborah's ancient song of victory in the early days of Israel: "From heaven fought the stars, from their courses they fought against Sisera." With all odds against them, the Israelites finally vanquished forces which threatened to conquer them. The heroine was keen enough to acknowledge that more than their weapons, strategy, and strength got them the victory. She was certain that this is the kind of world in which evil eventually runs out of bounds and is destroyed by God's moral order. It has not been put into dependable movements like the stars— and, we may add, like electrons in atomic structure.

Man can put something destructive, evil, and unlovely into orbit in his life. The earth may be seared, lives may be hurt, and cities destroyed while mad dictators flash across the horizon of history. The momentary triumph of evil may blind us to God's stars, symbols of the invincibility of truth and righteousness.

Yet God's stars illumine the faith that anything which would endure must be in tune with the "music of the spheres" or else will find its evil discords shattered by the infinite Creator. God's righteousness is as dependable as the path of the stars; his love is greater than their number; his judgment is as certain as their light in the dark. That which serves evil will, in God's good time, find the immutable laws of life fighting against it.

Stars are a sure guide when the night is clear. By their light travelers and mariners have been guided home. Only the foolish would discount and ignore God's lanterns because clouds sometimes hide their brightness. Neither will he who walks by faith ignore the light and constellations of truth and love because for a moment "we see darkly." Faith remembers the verdict of the clear nights by which all of life may be realigned and set.

A star also shone over Bethlehem when Jesus was born. Brightest is that star which leads to the Life in which our lives find a holy course and behold the brightness of God's grace. When the Savior becomes the center of the orbit of our faith and living, we will sing and rejoice with the mornings stars.

*   *   *

From heaven fought the stars, from their courses they fought against Sisera (Judges 5:20).

SCRIPTURE READING: Philippians 2:14-18

PRAYER: O God our Father who hast continued to rule beyond every proud victory of evil and hast ordained that thy righteousness and love in Christ shall abide, grant that in every darkness we may look unto those who have courageously followed and trusted thee. May we let kindness and truth illumine our course among the lives of others; through Jesus Christ our Lord. Amen.

AUTUMN FLIGHT

When the last days of autumn's smothered sunshine linger pensively, the spirit of flight is in the air. The many-hued leaves are lifted by the wind and flutter helplessly to the ground. Swallows and red-winged blackbirds begin to flock impulsively on bush and tree. The horizons are etched in haze until frost time. Then with the cold, clear, long view comes the awakening of an instinctive longing within the breast of the large and the small birds. They heed the mysterious warning of the approaching winter and fly southward to unseen climes where the sun tarries warm and long.

Foremost expressions of the migratory instinct are the drifting "V" formations of the wild geese flying high. Their high-pitched honking, alternatingly clear and then faint, carried by the shifting breeze, quickens the pulse. One is conscious of not possessing wings. Yet our imagination accompanies their flight, and we wonder what wilderness they came from and where they will find refuge. In the daytime the eye follows them until the last speck is lost in the blue skies. In the night ears are strained until the final garbled notes mingle with the echo of recollections. "Something whispered, 'Snow'"* to the wild geese.

Something beyond instinct and winter warning whispers to us of lonesomeness and stirs our soul to restlessness. As

---

*From "Something Told the Wild Geese" by Rachel Field in *Branches Green*. Copyright The Macmillan Co. 1934, renewed 1962 by Arthur S. Pederson. Used by permission.

we create and love, dream and sing, struggle and aspire, we can see some of the things we have built or established. Yet sadly we also look for a beauty and goodness which have eluded us. Our conscience complains that our will is sluggish. In the next moment we may have visions and dreams which need more than a lifetime to achieve. What is this discontent within the heart of man which mingles wistfully with a mysterious homing instinct to reach out beyond time and space to commune with the Infinite One? The psalmist does not explain it, but he describes something of this spiritual autumn flight: "My soul longs, yea, faints for the courts of the Lord; my heart and flesh sing for joy to the living God. Even the sparrow finds a home, and the swallow a nest for herself where she may lay her young, at thy altars, O Lord of hosts" (Psalm 84:2-3).

To call one species of wild fowl the "Canadian goose" is to describe only a portion of its habitat and flight. It belongs to both the northern and the southern climate. To name man as a creature of the earth, is to overlook what he feels himself to be in moments of highest inspiration. Our labels range all the way from business man to laborer, from scientist to artist. But they do not fathom the "homing instinct" and the sense of destiny in a man's soul. When we know ourselves as a child of the human race and as a child of God, then we look "forward to the city which has foundations, whose builder and maker is God" (Heb. 11:10).

Occasionally a lone goose will linger on a lake after the others have left for the south. Perhaps it is bewildered or afraid. The waters surrounding the goose eventually freeze

and close in until its legs are in hopeless grip. Then wolves or the cold bring death. There is a season in everyone's life when good flying time must be heeded before it is too late. We dare not wait too long with choices between the wrong and the right, the evil and the good or our postponement of a decision is to decide that we remain where we are. Then something else takes matters in hand, and we can no longer determine the outcome. A Christian decides the zones in which he can best be used of God. "A man's life does not consist in the abundance of his possessions" (Luke 12:15b).

We are born on this earth like fledglings which glimpse life in the northland, the earth. There comes a time in life as well as in death when we must take our first flight "southward." We may trust Christ's leading through joy and pain, sacrifice and death. After Easter all who felt his presence in their heart knew that he possessed the wings of eternity. Through his "resurrection and life" we know the joy of citizenship in two worlds and "our dwelling place in all generations."

        ✿   ✿   ✿

Even the stork in the heavens knows her times; and the turtle-dove, swallow and crane keep the time of their coming; but my people know not the ordinance of the Lord (Jer. 8:7).

SCRIPTURE READING: Philippians 3:12-21

PRAYER: Almighty and everlasting God, who hast entrusted unto us the yearning for life eternal, may not the things of the earth limit us, may not our sight of the earth blind us, may not the sounds of the earth keep us from hearing thy voice until we reach our eternal home; through Jesus Christ our Lord. Amen.

WATCHERS FOR TOMORROW

The raging, leaping flames of a forest fire fill the heart of man and of animal with terror. Driven by wind, the racing inferno sears thousands of acres of valuable timber and erases beauty and life from the ravished earth for many years. Sometimes the fires are ignited by lightning. Other holocausts can be attributed to a few careless tourists and campers, hunters and fishermen. Usually they are unaware that their failure to extinguish flames and embers causes this inestimable damage to wood, wildlife, and beauty. They fail to see for tomorrow the consequences of their careless enjoyment today.

Fortunately there are those who are watchers for tomorrow. In tall towers, overlooking the countryside, observers may be found during the dry, pregnable seasons searching for the first spiral of smoke signaling a potential conflagration. Occasionally an airplane will soar overhead, indicating that watchfulness reaches to far horizons. Others are working unseen as they set out young trees, stock lakes, open trails, and guard against ruthless human predators, violating the normal season and rhythm of wild life. These alert observers are interested in conserving and developing the

133

resources and potentials of forest and stream for generations to come.

Watchers for tomorrow may also appear in the identity of happy, thoughtful campers seeking the inspiration of woodland and waterways. They gather firewood from dry or fallen trees without mutilating living growth. They will not rob others of beauty in the surrounding setting. Some additional firewood is stacked, and the campsite is left in neat order for those who have waited long and have journeyed far.

The essence of reverent handling of life and of its enjoyment stems from two religious insights. One is illustrated by the beautiful tribute: "The earth is the Lord's and the fulness thereof" (Psalm 24:1a). Watchers for tomorrow are aware that no one can really appropriate or "own" the earth even though he may have title to the land or may have paid for the cost of his vacation. To use selfishly or to destroy anything God has entrusted to us does not make it more our own. It is lost for everyone in the days to come. What happens to a deer or a grouse, a tree or a wild flower, is important in the light of him to whom everything belongs. The beauty, the resources, and the delight are ours to appreciate for a brief, swift day. At evening time we return everything beneath the mantle of the night to its Creator. Upon awakening the light reveals the gifts and trust of a new day which was yesterday's "tomorrow."

Not only does the earth and its fulness belong to God but also "those who dwell therein" (Psalm 24:1b). This awareness determines the manner in which we look upon those who will come down the trails today and tomorrow. The spirit of conserving the fullness of the earth and that of seeking to enrich the life of our fellow "dwellers" is nourished by the recognition that the coming generations, as well as we, belong to the Eternal One. Our giant corporations, mighty civic enterprises, huge cities, and tremendous crowds tend to make our life impersonal. Yet it is the awareness of the worth of the individual which preserves the values in all relationships for tomorrow.

In the intimacy of the family we handle each other's possessions with care and respect because we honor one another. The acknowledgment of "God's ownership" and of "God's family" is a fundamental part of religious experience. The Christian church has looked upon her members as a "family of faith" and as a "family in blessings." The sense of "membership" one with another is an outgrowth of a healthy Christian faith. The church would release us from restricted ties and would broaden and deepen our concern. Out of these bonds of faith comes a spirit which hallows all other relationships in city and country, for the individual and for society, making us true watchers for tomorrow.

*   *   *

You are not your own; you were bought with a price (2 Cor. 6:19b-20a).

SCRIPTURE READING: Psalm 24

PRAYER: Eternal God, who withholdest no good things from thy children, grant us the spirit of reverence as we receive blessings by which our souls are inspired, our bodies are strengthened, and our minds are enriched. Help us to be good stewards of the gifts thou hast entrusted to us for generations to come; through Jesus Christ our Lord. Amen.

KEY VERSES AND SCRIPTURE READINGS

Title	*Key Verse*	*Scripture Reading*
Trailblazers	Heb. 11:8	Gen. 12:1-8
Silence	Mark 6:31	1 Kings 19:9-12
Thunder and Lightning	John 3:17	Job 28:25-28
		Rom. 11:33-36
Beauty After the Rain	Eccl. 3:11	Ps. 19:1-10
Ahead of Us	Ps. 21:3	Ps. 23
Watchers for Tomorrow	1 Cor. 6:19b-20a	Ps. 24
Like an Eagle	Isa. 40:31,	Ps. 91
A Psalm of Nature	Ps. 150:6	Ps. 100
		Acts 16:25-28
Sunrise and Sunset	Rev. 4:8b	Ps. 113:1-6
Elf Tracks	Matt. 18:3	Isa. 35:1-4
Little Creatures	Matt. 6:30	Matt. 6:25-33
The Unlocked Door	Matt.. 25:35	Matt. 25:31-46
Scars	Gal. 6:17	Matt. 27:27-31
Wonders in Miniature	Luke 16:10	Mark 4:30-32
The Twisted Pine	Luke 4:18a	Luke 4:18-30
The Cache	Mark 8:36	Luke 12:16-21
Winds of Chance	Rev. 19:6b	Luke 13:1-9
Driftwood	Luke 15:24	Luke 15:11-24
The Well	John 4:14	John 4:7-26
Puff-Balls	Mark 8:35	John 15:12-17
Skylines in the Night	Heb. 12:1b-2a	Rom. 5:1-5
The Cry of the Wild	Rom. 8:16	Rom. 8:12-17
Indian Paintings	2 Cor. 3:2	Rom. 10:12-17
The Lure of Islands	Rom. 12:5	Rom. 12:1-8
Design for Survival	Phil. 1:27-28a	1 Cor. 1:22-31
A Double Rainbow	Rev. 2:10	1 Cor. 11:23-28
The Ridge Pole	Ps. 51:6	Gal. 6:1-10
Storm-Felled	Eph. 3:17b-19a	Eph. 6:10-17
Parasites	Phil. 2:3	Phil. 2:4-11
The Stars in Their Courses	Judges 5:20	Phil. 2:14-18
Autumn Flight	Jer. 8:7	Phil. 3:12-21
Priceless Treasures	Isa. 55:1-2	Phil. 4:4-9
Reflected Images	Gen. 1:27	Col. 3:8-15
Pine Cones	Dan. 12:3	1 Tim. 4:7-12
A Trip into the Wilderness	1 Tim. 6:11	1 Tim. 6:9-12
Riding with the Waves	Phil. 4:12-13	2 Tim. 2:1-13
A Landing Place	John 1:42	Heb. 4:14-16
Fog	Heb. 11:1	Heb. 11:1-6
Beauty Within	1 Peter 2:5	1 Peter 2:4-10
A Borrowed Light	1 John 4:19	1 John 4:17-21